A Vision of Victory
on Earth as in Heaven

A 21st Century Commentary on the Book of Revelation

Robert L. McCan, Ph.D.

Quantity discounts may be available for educational purposes, bulk sales, and group study.

Contact the author, Robert L. McCan at 513 West Broad Street, Suite 517, Falls Church, Virginia 22046 or through his website: www.BobMcCan.com.

ISBN-13: 978-1492903055

LCCN: 2013919912

Published by Flying Swan Publications, Fairfield, Iowa, USA.

COVER ART

The book of Revelation is so rich with images, it is challenging to choose only a few.

The breathtaking Hubble telescope images of space reveal vast galaxies and universes, even within the apparently dark areas of our night sky. This objective "revelation" blesses us in the 21st century with an awareness of the unfathomable scale of God's creative power, commensurate with the realizations of accomplished mystics of earlier times, such as the author of Revelation.

In Revelation, the angels and elders sing unceasing praises to God around His throne (Revelation 4:8-11, 5:13-14, 7:11-15, 11:15-18, 15:2-4). Alas, we did not find a way to directly represent this "great company of heaven" in our cover art without undue anthropomorphizing.

The Tree of Life by the river of the waters of life, with leaves for the healing of the nations, comes from Revelation 22:1-2. The branches of the Tree reach into heaven, while its roots anchor into the earth.

The symbol of the lion lying down with the lamb has several layers of meaning. Perhaps most profoundly it can represent apparently opposite but actually paradoxical attributes of the Divine. In Revelation, Christ is called both the "Lion of…Judah" (5:5) and the "Lamb" (5:6, 7:17, 14:10, 15:3, 19:9, 21:23; 22:1). In Christ are harmonized both the indomitable, ferocious courage and strength of the Lion and the absolute purity, innocence, and harmlessness of the Lamb.

DEDICATION

This book is dedicated to Peggy McCan, my wife, who since a small child has thrilled at the magnificent vision of angels and archangels singing glorious anthems around the throne of God.

"Therefore, with Angels and Archangels, and with all the company of heaven, we laud and magnify Thy glorious Name; evermore praising Thee...."

The Great Thanksgiving,
The Holy Communion Rite One,
The Book of Common Prayer

Table of Contents

PREFACE

He was the meekest and lowliest of all the sons of men, yet he spoke of coming on the clouds of heaven with the glory of God. He was so austere that evil spirits and demons cried out in terror at his coming, yet he was so genial and winsome and approachable that the children loved to play with him, and the little ones nestled in his arms. His presence at the innocent gaiety of a village wedding was like the presence of sunshine.

No one was half so compassionate to sinners, yet no one ever spoke such red hot scorching words about sin. A bruised reed he would not break, his whole life was love, yet on one occasion he demanded of the Pharisees how they ever expected to escape the damnation of hell. He was a dreamer of dreams and a seer of visions, yet for sheer stark realism he has all of our stark realists soundly beaten. He was a servant of all, washing the disciples' feet, yet masterfully he strode into the temple, and the hucksters and moneychangers fell over one another to get away from the mad rush and the fire they saw blazing in his eyes.

He saved others, yet at the last himself he did not save. **There is nothing in history like the union of contrasts which confronts us in the gospels. The mystery of Jesus is the mystery of divine personality.**

James Stewart (1896-1990)

There is no greater drama in human record than the sight of a few Christians, scorned or oppressed by a succession of emperors, bearing all trials with a fierce tenacity, multiplying quietly, building order while their enemies generated chaos, fighting the sword with the Word, brutality with hope, and at last defeating the strongest state that history has ever known. **Caesar and Christ had met in the arena and Christ had won.**[1]

Will Durant

---

1 Durant, Will, Caesar and Christ (in the series *The Story of Civilization*), Simon and Schuster, 1944, p. 652.

INTRODUCTION

The last book of the bible has always captured my interest. As a child in a conservative Southern Baptist church in a small mid-western town, I heard snatches of terrifying predictions of doom from ministers and visiting evangelists. At the same time I was also treated to beautiful pictures of paradise. I was, over all, introduced to a God of love and a compassionate Jesus who cared for the last and the least among us. The dire calamities and the tender invitations in Revelation made little sense—until as a graduate student in theology and ethics at the theological college of the University of Edinburgh, Scotland, I had the opportunity to study Revelation in some depth with a great scholar, a deeply devout Christian, and the best preacher I have had the privilege to know. Dr. James Stewart, Professor of New Testament, wrote many books, guided a generation of student ministers, and served as chaplain to Queen Elizabeth II.

As minister of the First Baptist Church of Clarksville, Tennessee in the 1950s, I took on the challenge of preparing 13 expository sermons that covered the entire content of Revelation from the first to the 22nd chapters. These sermons were then published by Broadman Press (the official Southern Baptist press) as a book of sermons titled ***A Vision of Victory***. Many years later my daughter Mary was a librarian at the

Washington Theological Union, a consortium of several Roman Catholic Seminaries in the greater Washington, D.C. area. My interest in a deeper study of Revelation grew as she brought me books on the topic from their extensive collection. In the next twenty years, my reflections have further matured, and I feel they are now ready for sharing.

I do not approach this challenge lightly. I recognize the presence of "holy mystery" and the need for humility by me, and indeed, by all who deal with the book.

As my own study and reflection matured I came to understand the amazing mysteries of Revelation and how the book is, in fact, humanity's ultimate vision of victory. John, the author, believed this completion was possible because of the relationships among the hosts in heaven and the human beings on earth. This cosmic community includes not only Jesus, the Son, but also the angelic hosts, the saints of heaven, the churches with their clear mission, individual faithful Christians with their witness, and finally, the whole human family that join their hands and voices. God is not ready or willing to exercise His ultimate power until all of the other actors in this drama are ready to do their part. All combine their energy and skill in a great circle of love to chain Satan and cast him into a bottomless pit so that humanity can at last fully love God and each other and live abundantly in the divine harmony that God willed from the beginning of creation!

To whom is my book addressed? I write especially to Christians who are willing to invest in study and serious reflection to unlock a significant level of this mystery and understand its marvelous message. My audience is primarily educated, science-based Christians in "mainline" Protestant denominations and in the Roman Catholic Church. Few teachers and ministers or priests from these churches try to engage their members or the larger Christian community with the message of Revelation. Yet, so many Bible school educated, self-taught evangelists have flooded the airwaves and preached perversions of this message. I believe there is none among us who will not profit greatly from this study. My goal is to bring this amazing book to life in simple language and to clarify its complex visions into shining truths.

Revelation is a complex book. The author, John, had a brilliant mind. He was a profound scholar who was steeped in Hebrew scripture. Further, he was a prophet who understood the political issues facing the Christian community. But he was more. John was a theologian/ philosopher whose mind soared to consider the beginning and ending of history and the ultimate nature of good and evil. He chose to place Jesus, known as "the Christ," as the focal point of that history, and then he explained how this unfolded. He dealt with specific issues of justice in his time, but his mind also soared to a consideration of the meaning of justice in human history. He ultimately affirmed God's eternal love as more powerful than all the forces of evil. He challenged Christians of all ages, including ours, to lives of devotion and service. He believed there is a realm where God reigns beyond this world, from which we can gain inspiration and strength to remain steadfast in devotion and service in the face of seemingly overwhelming obstacles. John also reignited the mission of Jesus by envisioning the contributions of all the members of God's cosmic community for building the kingdom of God "on earth as it is in heaven."

We study the book verse by verse, and where it merits, word by word. We also discuss how it was understood historically and among those with differing interpretations. At the conclusion of each chapter there is a section titled, "This I Believe" in which I present my conclusions along with my reasons for them. At every point I show the implications for our personal lives and for our society. Finally, the chapters end with questions for group discussion. But before we turn to a study of the book itself, it will be helpful to consider the nature of paradox that pervades the book of Revelation and alternative views of the basic nature of John's visions.

The Mystery of Paradox

A major stumbling block in understanding Revelation is contained in what I choose to call "the mystery of paradox." One such paradox, for example, is in the dual concepts of God as Love, personified as the all-loving Father, versus God as a destructive, wrathful avenger. Indeed, many modern and post-modern Christians naturally resist and recoil from the many destructive apocalyptic images in Revelation that our more fundamentalist cousins appear to directly engage, if not actually relish.

Can these opposite concepts of God be reconciled? Must we conclude that if one is true the other is false? Near the end of Revelation we have a portrait of a New Jerusalem with twelve gates always open to welcome the people and tribes and nations of earth in a glorious homecoming! Yes, they must "wash their robes" to cleanse themselves from evil. But all are welcome. "The Spirit and the bride say, 'Come.' And let everyone who hears say, 'Come.' And let everyone who is thirsty come. Let anyone who wishes take the water of life as a gift." (Revelation 22:17) But just prior to that picture is one of Jesus descending from heaven riding the white horse and carrying a huge sickle, cutting down the inhabitants of earth in the ultimate expression of God's wrath. (Revelation 14:14-20)

Another paradox depicts the earth as becoming ever more evil until nothing good prevails. Then Christ comes again in glory and brings life on earth to an end. Only heaven and hell remain. Yet again, Revelation and the New Testament generally depict an everlasting kingdom on earth which becomes so filled with God's love and our love for each other that the kingdom on earth finally becomes a full expression of God's kingdom in heaven. Christ has come, and his glory fills the earth! The prophet Habakkuk predicted this kingdom when he wrote, "But the earth will be filled with the knowledge of the glory of the Lord, as the waters cover the sea." (Habakkuk 2:14)

How do we approach these paradoxes? An obvious response is to say that these contradictions cannot be reconciled. At best, one of these concepts is false. But others see a deeper truth in the paradox. They see truth on both sides that must be expressed. Precisely because God is love, God cannot tolerate injustice. The one unfairly treated is also a person dear to God. God cannot forever permit a powerful Caesar to persecute Christians because of their faithful witness to Christ. God must ultimately destroy systems of unjust laws and social customs that keep some in poverty or servitude by enriching others at their expense. The outcasts are also children of God, equally loved by God. So, God's challenge is to express His deepest love and have it ultimately prevail for all people. For this to happen, the systems that have oppressed God's people and damaged God's creation on earth—whether through human ignorance, shortsightedness, or outright greed and evil—must be destroyed.

There are certain laws of nature inherent in God's creation. God has made human beings in His/Her image and endowed us with free will and the ability to learn and grow from our experience. We learn and grow much more gracefully and joyfully when we maintain our connection with God and embed our lives in His/Her love and power. If human beings, out of ignorance and/or evil, exploit each other and the earth for selfish gain at others' expense, the natural consequences are the kinds of things we see in our world today—the many forms of social and economic injustice, worsening environmental degradation with ever more destructive weather patterns, etc. These are natural consequences of human action, not arbitrary punishment by God, though it can be interpreted as punishment or revenge through a particular kind of religious lens.

Many other cultures do not have such a hard time acknowledging the destructive face of God. In the Vedic scripture the *Bhagavad Gita,* for example, Lord Krishna (an incarnation of the Divine) teaches Arjuna (one of the greatest warriors of his time) in preparation for a great battle between the forces of good and evil. Arjuna, though he sees the necessity for the battle, does not want to engage in it, because the evildoers on the other side are also his relatives, former friends, and mentors with their own greatness. During the instruction, Arjuna asks Lord Krishna to reveal to him his Divine (rather than human) form. Lord Krishna reveals himself, and Arjuna sees the entire scope of the functioning of the Divine—giving birth to new galaxies, universes, populations, and worlds while also devouring and destroying any and all creations eventually over the vast expanse of time. Arjuna cannot tolerate this expanded vision of the Divine for any length of time and begs Krishna to restore the veil to his eyes. Yet, this glimpse of the unfathomable, multifaceted totality of God's nature served as part of Krishna's teaching to Arjuna. This brief vision helped empower Arjuna to do his part as a warrior with compassion and integrity to restore righteousness at his particular time in history.

The apocalyptic aspect of the book of Revelation is the primary place in the New Testament where we glimpse this full range of the Divine, with the paradox of creation and destruction working together toward a fuller expression of the Divine in the world. Ultimately, creation and destruction, like the values of love and justice, support each other. Love finally prevails in the context of human freedom, if human beings can align themselves with Divine law (justice), love, and power exercised in the interests of those values.

It is instructive to note that the book of Revelation does not contain the word "vengeance." In fact the word is used only four times in the New Testament and two of these are references to the verse in Deuteronomy (32:35), "Vengeance is mine...." However, there are seven references to the "wrath of God" in Revelation. This can be understood, not as vengeance or punishment, but as an ultimately merciful clearing away of the life-damaging structures and evil powers that prevent the realization of the Kingdom of God on earth.

This is the mystery of Jesus described by James Stewart in our Preface. As Niels Bohr, father of modern quantum physics, said in regard to the nature of the universe, "There are trivial truths and great truths. The opposite of a trivial truth is plainly false. The opposite of a great truth is also true."

At the heart of both the scientific universe and the universe of scripture we are confronted by "holy mystery." The great truths of paradox invite us into the mystery at the depths of the Divine nature, even if we do not yet see "face to face." We gain understanding by appreciating the truth in both sides of a paradox, but the ultimate reality is a mystery, which we of the Christian faith choose to call Divine mystery.

Visions as Literal Reality or Literary Device?

Are John's visions presented as literary metaphors and symbols, giving deeper meaning to the experiences of the early Christians by relating them to traditional Hebrew Scriptures? Or, are they in some way descriptions of actual events, with angels in heaven singing around the luminous throne of God, and with incense rising under the altar to herald the prayers of the saints on earth? What about the beast with seven heads and ten horns, the serpent, or the mighty dragon swatting a third of the stars from the sky with a tremendous sweep of its tail? Much is metaphor. What, if anything, is literal?

This is surely a literary vision. The vast majority of the words, concepts, visions, and images are taken directly from Hebrew scripture. Yes, there are also myths and stories from the first century culture of John's time, representing fears embedded deep in the psyche of the masses of people in the Roman world of that time and indeed, some fears peculiar to the Christian community, based on prior persecutions and current threats.

There is much to digest for the 21st century Christian who accepts both faith and science. We gain perspective when we realize that everything in Revelation is related to its central theme of providing hope and courage for Christians of the author's time caught in persecution—and Christians of every time engaged in the great work of trying to build the kingdom of heaven on earth against all odds.

Beyond a literary form of expression, was John also rising to a level of perception of spiritual reality unavailable to most persons unless they apply themselves to intense meditation and other spiritual practices? Can mystics cultivate over time the ability to hear the music of heaven and see celestial (and demonic) beings on a more subtle level of creation? Was John given a mystical vision that expressed reality deeper than words can convey? Did heaven's door open so he could actually see inside? Did he enter the real presence of God? Did he actually see Jesus, the Son, worshipped and glorified?

I present two views in addition to my own. The first is the summary of an article in *The Christian Century* magazine (May 29, 2013) by Sara Maitland[2], titled "The Perils of Silence." She experienced long periods of "radical silence" herself and has studied human reaction to such silence. She notes classic symptoms of psychosis in those who live in this radical silence. "The oddest of these are auditory hallucinations: hearing voices in silence is a widely reported experience that has very little to do with the reasons why someone is silent." Indeed, some have considered John's visions to be borderline psychotic hallucinations brought about by the isolation and the privations of imprisonment.

---

[2] She is the author of *From the Forest: A Search for the Hidden Roots of Our Fairy Tales,* Counterpoint Press.

Sara Maitland recalls her own experience. She wrote, "I have sat in silence in a windstorm and listened (not without pleasure) to a male voice choir singing in Latin." She attributes for most people hearing voices to a quirk in the brain. "I think that rather than being sudden and isolated instances of insanity, these voices are instances of the normal human brain exercising itself in the absence of its ordinary task—breaking up human speech."

Sara Maitland sees three types of experience in committed silence, all found in the writings of Teresa of Avila. First, there is the true enlightening mystical experience with its many variations. Despite her skepticism, Sara Maitland does not exclude the possibility of authentic mystical visions in which the seeker finds the living God. That is different from a similar experience caused by radical silence among others who are not seekers after God. Experiences of the demonic can also break through when the human psyche is troubled, with the mind devolving to its most elemental level of cold blooded creatures (dragons and snakes), causing terror rather than ecstasy. Finally, there is madness for those who cannot manage the experience of aloneness.

My other example of a witness to silence and mystical experience available through deep meditation is from my daughter, Susanna, who is also the editor for this book. Susanna spent years in intensive meditation courses in the Transcendental Meditation movement and studied a variety of religions and cultures in addition to her native Christianity. She described an experience: "One thing that happened to me when I was doing the very long meditations was that I heard what sounded like choirs of angels singing in 32-part harmony for extended periods of time. Even though this was an unexpected side-effect of the meditation, I am aware that people in similar circumstances throughout the ages report similar experiences. So perhaps there is some sort of 'reality' to it. Or in Jungian terms, people may have similar experiences of certain archetypes of the collective unconscious, even though these experiences may be colored by their individuality or their cultural perspectives."

About another experience she wrote, "Once in an advanced Chi Gong class my subtle sense of sight opened up and I saw what looked like luminous white clouds swirling around the room. This fit the traditional description of what that level of 'chi' or life energy can look like. Hence, when I read something in Revelation like 'Behold, he is coming with the clouds,' (Revelation 1:7) it makes complete sense to me, and a vision of angels wrapped in clouds or sitting on clouds makes complete sense. That is simply what it looks like to anybody who happens to have the eyes to see it at a particular time, because they are what John would call 'in the spirit.'"

Susanna notes that until recent centuries most Christians, and many others, believed in angels and attributed some sort of reality to the heavenly realm. They saw it as a level of existence subtler than material, earthly life. Heaven and earth were understood to be interrelated. Angels were understood to be light beings who, as messengers and agents of God's will, can interact with human beings, giving insight, inspiration, guidance, healing and protection. Similarly, Jesus Christ and the saints were thought to be living in a reality on this subtler level of creation, united with or in the immediate Presence of the Godhead, continuing to guide the Church and pour out Divine grace on the world.

Many Christians believed over the centuries that, with the Grace of God, perhaps facilitated by fasting and prayer, one could gain experiential access to this level of life. Mystics such as Theresa of Avila and others gained varied and detailed knowledge and experience of these realms. Was the perception of people who were culturally open to these levels of creation more developed in this dimension than we are, when we limit ourselves exclusively to the modern "scientific" version of reality?

Susanna notes further, "In the heavenly realms, beings appear in forms that more accurately express their true inner nature—the nature of their attitudes and behavior. For example, an oppressive emperor driven by greed and a lust for power might appear on a subtler level in a reptilian form, as a dragon, because he is functioning on the basis of primitive predatory instincts, still present in human beings as the older 'reptilian' parts of the brain and nervous system. In contrast, the angels appear radiant and beautiful because they are imbued with Divine light and see with Divine wisdom."

I present these examples of others' experiences and understandings not to try to convince readers of the "reality" of other levels of experience, but simply to expand readers' sense of possibility and appreciation of the mysteries that exist beyond ordinary human understanding. It is certainly not necessary to believe in any kind of quasi-objective reality of John's visions in order to derive full benefit from our study of Revelation.

In the same spirit, throughout this book I will be offering several vantage points from which to consider Revelation, most of which are not mutually exclusive. I will also offer my own conclusions and beliefs about the issues raised in Revelation, not to persuade readers to adopt my beliefs, but to encourage readers to engage these issues for themselves at a deeper level than they may have before.

This I Believe

Each of us faces a profound choice at the deepest level. We can accept by faith a scientific view of human life that chooses to exclude God and the spirit realm, or we can, again by faith and as scientists, accept God, even a God whose love for humanity is all-encompassing. (We recognize this "leap of faith" as one that science can neither prove nor disprove.) We can then quite readily take the next step and posit heaven and, yes, God's providence over life and history. We can then explore what Susanna calls "the subtle realm" of angels and the nature of life after death. I am ready to take this leap of faith, believing it makes more sense than the alternative. I have had only limited personal experiences where another world has opened to me. I live into an acceptance of "holy mystery" and recognize that all ultimate things are beyond human expression. I study the book of Revelation and catch glimpses into a heavenly realm while recognizing that it is presented in human terms for my understanding.

In addition to Revelation, I find entry to heaven through gifted musicians who are able to hear the "music of the spheres." They hear angelic choirs and capture that divine music for an earthly audience. When inspired music is performed by musicians who appreciate the deep purpose of what they are doing, the music has the power to resonate on a celestial level and create for human listeners powerful and sublime experiences such as those described in Revelation. Handel's Messiah, for example, was believed to have been written under such divine inspiration, and much of the text comes from Revelation. I feel power and inspiration from these inspired works of art and sense a level of "reality" that I cannot entirely understand.

My spirit resonates with the mighty music of Benjamin Britten, who also wrote the words: "For the TRUMPET of God is a blessed intelligence and so are all the instruments in HEAVEN. For God, the Father Almighty, plays upon the HARP of stupendous magnitude and melody. For at that time malignity ceases and the devils themselves are at peace. For this, time is perceptible to man by a remarkable stillness and serenity of soul."[3]

---

3 Rejoice In the Lamb. 1943.

I cannot discount the multiple and dynamic ways friends and other writers describe how they come into the presence of the divine and discern something of heaven. There are different doorways for different people. Some find God through the beauty and harmony of nature, or in loving other people, or in caring for the poor and dispossessed, or through the church's liturgy, or in corporate prayer.

Finally, my own appreciation grows for the words used weekly in the Episcopal liturgy in the expression "holy mysteries." I believe we are trying to put into words and pictorial images mysteries that most of us have very little concrete experience to describe. I believe that the words, the music and the pictorial scenes in heaven are given human expression in words and images familiar to John, the writer, but they point to mystery beyond human expression. The Apostle Paul aptly stated the matter, "...no eye has seen, no ear has heard, nor the human heart conceived what God has prepared for those who love him." (1 Corinthians 2:9)

What is heaven like? When love and power work together, we expect a masterpiece! Beyond that, we make our videos and write our plays. We point to our deepest hope and abiding faith that God is on the throne and God rules in history and throughout eternity. At times we hear the harmony of great music that soars to infinite meaning and power. We are grateful for the witness of mystics who have taken time to be silent and search for the living God. We listen with our deepest level of discernment for the heavenly voices to assist in showing us the way.

The door John gazed through into heaven is ajar for us now as we begin our study of the book of Revelation!

Chapter 1

THE FELLOWSHIP OF SUFFERING: CONTEXT

A young college professor, a victim of multiple sclerosis, spoke in our church. He described the nature of his illness and how through his suffering he had laid hold on a deeper meaning of life. "During the past year," he said, "I have become part of a fellowship of suffering. This illness has brought me close to all who suffer and sometimes has lifted me into the very presence of God." This moving testimony left few dry eyes among those of us present.

I share this experience to introduce you to fellow church members who lived in Asia Minor at about 90 A.D. They were the Christians to whom the book of Revelation was addressed. The Roman Emperor Domitian had issued a decree making it a crime of treason to name Jesus as Lord because he wanted to be worshipped as a god above all others. The heavy hand of the empire seemed ready to crush the churches. The author of Revelation was a prisoner on the Isle of Patmos. Many of those early Christians in the seven churches to whom it was written were destined to die as martyrs. Dr. James Stewart of Edinburgh, Scotland, the New Testament professor under whom I studied

Revelation, aptly said, "Without tears it was not written, and without tears it cannot be understood."

Scholarly insight can help us unlock the mysteries of Revelation and explain the symbolism, which has become strange and remote to us. However, when John wrote to lay persons and pastors of his time, his mode of expression was familiar. For them, the book was filled with allusions to Hebrew scripture and popular legends, and the readers understood how John applied them specifically to their situation.

In preparation for unlocking the mysteries that enshroud this book we set ourselves down in the world of these churches. We will need to understand the tradition of apocalyptic writing in previous centuries and then learn about the symbolism used. But first let's place Revelation in the context of the other books of the Bible.

The Last Book of the Bible

The Bible is a library of 66 books, but it can also be seen as a continuous story of God's dealing with wayward humanity over time. We divide the Bible into two parts: the "Old Covenant" (Old Testament) or Hebrew Bible and the "New Covenant" (New Testament), the additional Christian scripture. The Old Covenant was originally made between God and Abraham. It further unfolded through Moses at Mount Sinai when God gave the Ten Commandments to the Hebrew people. As a further expression of this Covenant, Christians and Jews believed that God continued to send leaders and prophets to the Hebrew people over the centuries. Later, Christians concluded that Jesus established a New Covenant through his life, death, and resurrection. The early Christian community, beginning with Peter (Acts 10) and continuing with Paul, recognized that this New Covenant extended beyond the Jewish community to the larger human family.

From another perspective we can divide the Bible into five parts. First is the story of creation found in Genesis, the first book of the Hebrew Bible. The second part is the story of how creation was spoiled by sin and rebellion against God. It tells how God created a people, Israel, to be His agents or witnesses. They were to bear the promise of salvation for the world, as revealed through the insight of prophets. The third phase of this drama is the New Testament gospels: Matthew, Mark, Luke and John. For Christians, this is the astounding good news of God coming to humanity in the person of Jesus. Part four is about the formation and expansion of the early church, from the book of Acts through the short epistle of Jude. The final section of the Bible—the book of Revelation—is both a continuation of the pastoral letters and a vision of the end of history. The world becomes "…the kingdom of our Lord and of his Messiah, and he will reign forever and ever." (Revelation 11:15)

Sacred Scripture

I have come to believe that the book of Revelation should be revered as part of sacred scripture. But any student of church history knows that the book was not readily accepted as part of the canon. Its mysterious language and its harsh and apparently vengeful tone seemed to be unlike the nature and spirit of Jesus. Others recognized it as part of a broad category of writings called "Apocalyptic." The word "apocalypse" means "revelation of the divine purpose." The word implies an unveiling of hidden truth. Though controversial, the book gained a wide circulation and gradually became accepted as authoritative.

A number of prominent early church bishops and scholars accepted Revelation as part of the canon. Melito, Bishop of Sardis, (date of birth unknown, died 180 A.D.) first proposed the New Testament canon that was later adopted by the larger church. Clement of Alexandria (150-215 A.D.) had been educated in classical Greek philosophy and literature before his conversion to Christianity, and then taught theology at the university in Alexandria, Egypt. He believed the book of Revelation to be divinely inspired. Tertullian (160-225 A.D.), Bishop of Carthage, North Africa was another early church leader who included Revelation in the canon. Another was the great scholar, Irenaeus (130-202 A.D.), Bishop in what is now Lyon, France. Irenaeus was born and raised in Smyrna, where as a boy growing up he had listened to the sermons of Polycarp, Bishop of Smyrna. (Smyrna was one of the seven churches to whom Revelation was written.)

The first in the tradition of our modern apocalyptic fundamentalists was a second century preacher named Montanus. He taught that the church had entered its last days and predicted that Christ would come again and establish the New Jerusalem in his home town of Phrygia in Asia Minor. He and his sect based their rationale on certain verses in Revelation that he felt applied directly to himself. His followers uprooted their lives, left everything, and went to wait for the Lord's return. Subsequently, the sect was declared to be a heresy, and the book of Revelation fell out of favor with many churches.

On another side of the debate over whether Revelation was scripture was Gaius, an influential elder in the church in Rome. In 210 A.D. he wrote a manifesto declaring that Revelation was written by a Gnostic heretic and was not scripture. Later, in 250, Dionysius, Bishop of Alexandria, (died 265 A.D.), the first bishop to hold the designation of "Pope" in the Coptic Orthodox Church, made a careful study of the language and the grammar of Revelation and concluded it could not have been written by John the Apostle who wrote the gospel of John. Therefore, he concluded, it was not apostolic and, hence, should not be included in the canon. His careful study provided support for those who were concerned that some were wrongfully interpreting verses about the millennium and the last days in a literal way and were distorting the spiritual nature of Christianity by making extreme claims about end times.

As late as the fourth century, Eusebius, Bishop of Caesarea (263-339 A.D.), a noted church historian and theologian, classified competing books in an effort to decide which ones to include as scripture. He divided them into three categories: accepted, rejected, and disputed. He classified Revelation as disputed.

Making A Deal

Cyril of Jerusalem (315-386) omitted Revelation from his list of canonical books and forbade its use either publicly or privately. The Eastern Church raised serious questions about its inclusion and omitted it from the canon adopted at Laodicea in the fourth century. However, Revelation was included in the canon adopted in the West. After extended councils, the Western Church convinced those in the East to include it. A deal was struck to also include the book of Hebrews which had been accepted in the East but not in the West. Each convinced the other to accept the book in question.

Eleven centuries later Martin Luther included Revelation in his translation of the Bible but did not give it full canonical status because he felt it was inadequate theologically. He once called it "a book of straw" and said it had "as many mysteries as words." Zwingli, the Swiss Reformer in the era after Luther, pronounced it a "non-Biblical book" and John Calvin passed over it without comment, although he wrote a detailed commentary on all other New Testament books. Even today the lectionary of the Greek Orthodox Church (a branch of the Eastern Church) has no reading from Revelation.

I cite these historical references to show that making the canon was a slow and deliberate process that took more than 300 years to complete and may not have been entirely settled even at the time of the Reformation. The book of Revelation was the last book to gain general acceptance.

This I Believe

My own view is summarized in the opening words of the book of Revelation, that this is "the revelation of Jesus Christ." I have come to see God in Revelation as the same God who is Father of Jesus. Our God is not one-sided, like a doting grandfather who never lifts a finger against wickedness. The God of scripture is always one who judges sin. On one hand, this is the God of love, who seeks out and accepts sinners who repent and ask forgiveness. On the other hand, this is the God of justice, who metes out death for every cause that oppresses any part of humanity, turns them away from God, or harms the Church. Revelation makes clear both the goodness and mercy of God and the judgment against evil.

Will The Real Author Please Stand Up?

Who is the author of Revelation? We know that the author was John; we are not sure which John. "I, John, your brother..." could have been any one of several early church leaders about whom we have knowledge. The earliest traditional view was that the book was written by John the apostle. Generally, that was the position of the Western Church until about 240 A.D. The apostolic authorship was expounded by Justin Martyr (100-165 A.D.) who said the author was "a certain John, one of the apostles of Christ." Irenaeus referred to the author as "John, the disciple of the Lord who leaned on his breast at supper." The Eastern Church, however, challenged his authorship. Dionysius, Bishop of Alexandria, thought this book was so different from the Gospel of John that it could not have been written by the same man. He assigned authorship to John the Elder. R. H. Charles, a modern commentator,[4] was probably right when he assigned authorship to an unknown John, a Palestinian Jew, who immigrated to Asia Minor as an adult. He observed that the author of Revelation was thoroughly familiar with the Old Testament but wrote Greek very poorly.

Another contemporary scholar, M. Eugene Boring,[5] suggests that John probably fled to Asia Minor at the time of the fall of Jerusalem in 70 A.D., when there was a mass exodus of refugees. He feels that John's limited ability in Greek places his native language as either Hebrew or Aramaic (the language of Jesus). John was probably the bishop who had oversight of the seven churches to which he wrote.

As we progress through the book we shall see that John saw himself as a prophet, but not primarily one who predicted the future. In the lineage of Israel's prophets he was primarily concerned with interpreting current events. John had the mission of discerning the Lordship of Christ in the midst of the trials through which the church was passing.

---

[4] Charles, R. H., "The Revelation of St. John," *The International Critical Commentary*, (New York: Charles Scribner's Sons, 1920).

[5] Boring, M. Eugene, *Interpretation, A Bible Commentary for Teaching and Preaching Revelation* (Louisville: John Knox Press, 1989).

The book of Revelation is steeped in the Old Testament. Of the 404 verses, 278 point to specific Old Testament passages. Forty-five of these are from the book of Daniel. Yet there are few direct quotations. This leads me to assume that the author knew the Old Testament so well that it was second nature to him, but he did not have access to the scrolls from which to take quotations. John was a master of using brief Old Testament passages to convey enormous meaning.

From a study of the book we can infer that it was written by one in a position of leadership. He was part of the struggle about which he wrote and was well known to those in the seven churches, just as he had an intimate knowledge about each of these churches. John was a prisoner on the Isle of Patmos because of his faithfulness during the persecution. He was an inspired spokesman for God. Indeed, his message is a fitting climax to the great work of God in Christ Jesus.

The Historical Setting

The Jews in Palestine rebelled against Rome in the period between 66 and 70 A.D. Vespasian was Roman Emperor between 69 and 79 A.D. He dispatched his son, Titus, to put down the rebellion and disperse the population. As a result, the temple was destroyed, the city of Jerusalem was leveled, and Palestine was left in ruins. Untold thousands of freedom fighters were killed and a large population became refugees. They migrated to areas where Jewish people already lived, especially to Asia Minor. The

Jewish people were never to return to Palestine in significant numbers until the year 1948.

Asia Minor was the Roman province located on the western coast of what is now Turkey. Christian churches had been established across the region by Paul and his co-workers during the period from 50 to 60 A.D. The churches, therefore, had a Pauline tradition that was 30 to 40 years old by the time Revelation was written, probably in the early 90's during the reign of the Emperor Domitian (A.D. 81 to 96), a brother of the earlier warrior/ruler Titus. Paul, of course, shaped the development of the early churches and provided the theological underpinnings for taking the faith to the Gentile world.

Christian Immigrants Are Strange Strangers

These Christians to whom John wrote were a suspect group. Here was a new sect, mostly found among the poor immigrants to Asia Minor, although a substantial Jewish population had long lived there. They met for worship on a day that was not a public day of rest. Many people believed the Christians were unpatriotic. Most of them refused to honor the Emperor Domitian by placing incense on his altar as he required and saying, "Caesar is Lord." They spoke of eating flesh and drinking blood. But on the other hand, these same people were loving and caring, even though their leader had been crucified as a rebel decades earlier, an enemy to public order.

Thirty years earlier in Rome, the Emperor Nero had used Christians as scapegoats, accusing them of burning the city. Now Christians were being persecuted once more, this time for refusing to recognize and worship their Emperor Domitian as a god. Excavations in Ephesus, the largest metropolitan city of the province, have unearthed remains of a temple to Domitian with an enormous statue of the emperor. Fragments of the statue remain to this day.

The 90s was a time of prosperity for the middle and upper classes of Asia Minor, but the poor immigrants from Palestine benefited little and mostly remained poor. Worse, when Christians were taken to court for any reason, the opposing side would ask them to declare, "Caesar is Lord." When they refused, the judge would rule against them.[6] Those who conformed and said "Caesar is Lord" were given certificates exempting them from persecution.

When Revelation was written, persecution of the Christians was real but sporadic. The Christians feared that it would get worse and become systematic. This did not actually happen in that era. After Domitian's death the next Emperor decided to relax the demand for emperor worship. Nonetheless, for the next two hundred years Christians often faced discrimination, persecution and even martyrdom.

Why Was The Book Written?

Why was the book written, and what are the keys to its understanding? Some say the purpose of Revelation was solely to fortify the Christians caught in

---

[6] Hebrews 10:32-34; 12:3-4; 1 Peter 4: 12-16; 1 Peter 5:9-10

the throes of persecution. Its goal was to give courage to the martyrs.

Another school of thought believes the book was written to give Christians a blueprint for what to expect at the end of the world. Its purpose is to prophesy about the second coming of Christ, the final judgment, the last battle between Christ and Satan, and details of life in heaven. Many modern fundamentalists believe Revelation contains prophesy that provides a literal picture of things to come.

A subgroup of fundamentalists believes Revelation was written to provide an interpretation of reality for each period of history, as well as the final ending. They believe that prophesy is being fulfilled one chapter at a time, with perhaps each chapter representing a hundred-year span. Historical events are assigned to each vision. However the chapters are divided and assigned, most of these people believe that we are now living in the last days.

A final group of interpreters, mostly scholars, sees the book of Revelation as purely symbolic. It speaks of good and evil, victory and defeat, and the ultimate triumph of truth. This school of thought says it is a drama with a message, but it is fictional, to be understood without reference to its historical context.

This I Believe

I believe that the primary purpose of Revelation was to give courage to the martyrs and to interpret what was happening in the Roman world at that time in light of the Christian gospel. The might of the Roman Empire was pitted against small bands of Christians. This book of the Bible, like all others, must be understood against the backdrop of its historical setting.

Revelation is much more. It also tells us in broad terms about the end of history. We see by way of imaginative pictures that Christ will conquer every enemy. All things will be put under his feet. The forces of God and good will triumph, and God's children will live forever. Here is the ultimate victory and security for those early persecuted Christians, and, indeed, for us and all who follow in the train of history.

In similar fashion, Revelation deals with the world in each age as well as today. The warfare between God and Satan is being waged now. Christ is always in the midst of the churches. He is acting, directing and inspiring at this moment. Hence, there is always a contemporary application of the message.

But again, Revelation is not a timetable or step-by-step account of the rise and fall of nations and evil church leaders. It is not primarily a "futurist" book with a literal or detailed outline of events to come. There is nothing here, for example, about the rebirth of the state of Israel and the requirement of Christians to support Israel, based on Biblical prophecy.

A closer study presents the picture of a wonderful community of caring that proves to be more powerful than all opponents. The community is comprised of God, Jesus as Christ, the saints in heaven, the committed churches, the faithful individual

Christians, and the whole company of humanity. God is revealed to be unwilling to act unless or until all members of this community of caring are "on the same page." They will ultimately out-love and out-work and out-pray the forces of evil. When God sees that they are serious, He hears their pleas and answers their prayers. This insight is more critical than any timetable or prediction of specific events in history or at the end of time.

Symbols in Revelation

Finally, the book is full of symbols. These represent real life and actual people of that time, not just abstract ideas. The book uses these symbols as a semi-code. Christians who understood the code could read the message and discern its meaning, while enemies who might capture the scrolls would be dumbfounded.

One key to understanding Revelation is to recognize that the book is written in symbolic language. Our next task is to understand the meaning of the symbols.

Numbers as Symbols

Numbers as symbols pervade Revelation. The symbolic values of numbers were common knowledge among early Christians. Indeed, this kind of symbology had a long history among Jews and other peoples of the ancient world. Here is a list of the most commonly used numbers and their corresponding symbolic meanings:

1. ONE is the number of wholeness, completeness, as well as the first of the numbers.
2. TWO represents a division into opposite values in creative polarity.
3. THREE is the divine number. Father, mother and child make a family. God exists as Father, Son and Holy Spirit, (although God is not specifically described as Father, Son, and Holy Spirit in Revelation).
4. FOUR is the cosmic number, representing order in the world, the four cardinal directions—east, west, north and south—in relation to the sun. Houses and cities were usually built with four walls.
5. SEVEN is used more often than any other number. It occurs fifty-four times in Revelation. It consists of three plus four; the divine plus the world. Seven represents the completeness of the divine purpose in the world.
6. TEN represents human completeness. We have ten fingers and ten toes. The duty of humankind is summed up in the Ten Commandments. The millennium is 10 x 10 x 10 or the human completion of history, rather than a literal length of time.
7. TWELVE represents organized religion in the world. There were twelve tribes of Israel. It is no accident that Jesus chose twelve disciples. Twelve is four multiplied by three, the world times the divine.
8. SIX has a sinister meaning. It falls short of the sacred seven, which is perfection. Six represents

our inability to attain the ideal. Triple six is doom tripled. The number of the beast in Revelation is 666. It is evil raised to the nth degree.

These symbolic numbers were known and consciously used in ancient times. There are even unconscious carry-overs of these symbols into modern life. Our sense of time is still organized into seven days of the week and twelve months of the year. Our clocks still show a round of twelve hours. We still speak of the "four corners of the earth." The gambler tries to roll a "lucky seven" with the dice. The seventh inning of the baseball game is the time to stretch and expect special luck for the home team.

A Practical Pastoral Letter

Primarily, Revelation is a practical pastoral letter written to Christians in what is now Turkey to give them superhuman courage during their persecution. John did not intend to author a book of the Bible. Rather, he wrote a letter to his seven congregations, and he expected it to be read aloud during worship services. He addressed specific problems in the letter. John wrote because he had something important to say that he was not able to communicate in person. The curse of his separation from his fellow Christians was transformed into a blessing for Christianity as a whole, since this letter became the final book of the canon.

Like the other books of the New Testament, the gospel in Revelation was not revealed in philosophy or abstract essays but in the context of the continuing guidance of Jesus. It was revealed through finite persons struggling to respond to concrete situations while making relevant the good news (gospel) of Christ.

Revelation can be divided in various ways. At the most obvious level, Chapters 1-3 are direct messages to the seven churches. Chapters 4-18 are the vision of God's judgment against the emperor Domitian, who holds immense worldly power but is nonetheless revealed to be less powerful than Christ. This is the core theme, and specific imaginative pictures must be interpreted in light of this theme. Finally, Chapters 19-22 are a vision of the triumph of Christ and his bride the Church, the culmination of history with unspeakable glories for the faithful. I believe that the following verse is the best summary of the book of Revelation:

> "Be faithful until death,
> and I will give you the crown of life."
>
> Revelation 2:10 (b)

Apocalyptic Imagination

John meditated, used his imagination and/or had his vision, and crafted his letter in a popular literary pattern of his day. The book transmits a majestic, ecstatic vision of Christ, with angels and elders around the throne of God, but it also includes some horrific images of Satan, dragons, and every kind of vile beast. A closer look shows that the book is based on a lifetime of study and clear insight into the gospel. In fact, it is a literary vision in which John gathers a vast array of writings available both from scripture and other scrolls known to the author and to us. John arranges these writings, interprets them, and through their presentation provides a message that is his own, that is both unique and life-supporting. His soaring imagination expresses truth more profound than any dispassionate, logical essay could have conveyed.

Revelation is a book of imagination. It becomes bizarre and heretical only when taken literally. Truth is expressed with symbols and vivid imagery. Visions unfold in the mind's eye. I like to think of it as a music video with fast changing scenes.

As the Psalms are poetry and the book of Romans is a logical treatise, so Revelation makes its way to truth by using imagination. To grasp the deeper truth one must enter the art galleries or listen to the symphonies of heaven. One must experience reality more profound and holistic than logic. Beethoven had it right when he said, "Music is a higher revelation than philosophy." Or as Einstein said, "Imagination is more powerful than knowledge."

Chapter 2

CHRIST AMONG THE CHURCHES
Revelation 1

The profound message of Revelation for the Christian is that there is always victory beyond defeat. In this first chapter, we encounter churches subjected to persecution by agents of the Roman Emperor, Domitian. Some in these churches had already been martyred and the prospect was real for a widespread, systematic persecution. They were living through what they termed a "tribulation." But John said they would not be defeated if they were faithful. God is aware of their plight. He shares their suffering. Christ stands among the churches, present though unseen, and he holds their destiny in his hand.

The prophet on Patmos Island wrote in a dark hour and pointed to a light that cannot be extinguished. One summer day I was downtown during a storm. The sky began to grow black as the thunder rumbled. Then I began to notice lights burning on signs in front of stores and on billboards. I suddenly realized that these lights burn every day, but I had never noticed them when the sun was shining.

The night of persecution did not destroy the churches, but rather it made bright to the faithful the light of God's love. The dark days, seen through the lens of John's Revelation, helped intensify the devotion of the faithful.

This first chapter of Revelation teaches that Christ is building his kingdom through his Church. The Master organized a fellowship, the purpose of which was to transform the world. His Church is set down among frail, selfish and insecure people like us. The churches in Revelation were situated in an Empire that had an evil ruler. In addition, there were false teachers within the churches. Yet in the midst of warfare, oppression, and betrayal, Christ continued to build his Church. Indeed, the process continues today, and no outside force can stop it.

Now open your Bible (or click on your link!) and follow the commentary here based on Revelation Chapter 1.

Prologue to the Drama of Destiny (Revelation 1:1-3)

The book begins with a declaration that this is "the revelation of Jesus Christ." Scribes of a later era named it "The Revelation of John." Despite doubts and critics from the earliest days, this last book of the Bible was made a part of the New Testament canon precisely because the Church believed this to be "the revelation of Jesus Christ." If we choose to agree, the book not only invites our attention but demands our understanding.

The word "revelation" means to lay bare, to pull back the veil or curtain. One helpful way to view the book is to see it as a great allegorical drama. The curtain is pulled back, revealing the momentous events taking place in heaven. Every word in the book is John's own writing, most of it based on the words of other prophets and seers, yet it is John's vision that he is reporting. The first active verb in the first sentence, "...which God gave him," has God as the subject, just as did the first verse in Genesis.

John says that God made this vision known to him by "sending his angel" to him. The angel is a primary figure in apocalyptic literature,[7] and there are many references to angels in Revelation.[8] Angels are heavenly messengers. The message is to be shared. John bears witness; the Church is to continue that witness. "Blessed is he who reads aloud the words of the prophecy, and blessed are those who hear...." John has been a leader (bishop) in the churches to which he writes. He expects the letter to be read aloud in public worship. The act of reading aloud and hearing helps create and transmit the blessing to the people in the churches, just as saying the "I do" in a wedding ceremony helps to create the bonds of marriage.

"What must soon take place...the time is near." John expected the imminent return of Christ, just as

---

[7] Daniel 9:20-23

[8] There are more than 170 references to angels in Revelation. Among these are 1:1; 2:1; 5:11; 7:1; 8:6; 10:1; 15:1; 18:1; 19:9; 21:12; 22:8; 22:16

other Christians did throughout the first century. The persecution strengthened the conviction of Christians that the time was near. The entire book is filled with statements that depict the end of the world as being at hand. The saints in heaven are waiting and hoping for the end. They ask "how long?" and are told, "Wait a little longer."[9]

This I Believe

Does this mean that John was mistaken about the end of the world? Yes. He believed and wrote that the end was at hand. He was obviously mistaken. We revere the Bible as containing the Word of God, but we do not hesitate to acknowledge that the writers made mistakes. God used humans who were products of their times. When John adopted the apocalyptic mode of presentation he adopted its errors as well.

But the error in no way nullifies the message. It is wiser to follow the admonition of Jesus, "But of that day or that hour no one knows, not even the angels in heaven, nor the Son, but only the Father."[10] We do not know the times or seasons for the end. But we can share the sense of urgency felt by those who expected the immediate second coming of Christ. Our generation is the only one we have in which to do God's work.

---

[9] Revelation 6:10-11

[10] Mark 13:32

John says that he is testifying to the word of God and the testimony of Jesus Christ. For him there is no question but that this is a message the churches need to hear and heed. John writes to the seven churches in Asia. These are the churches located in a semi-circle over a hundred mile area with which he was intimately familiar. John had probably been the bishop or overseer of these churches.

Greetings (Revelation 1:4-8)

John used the same salutation employed by Paul in writing to these churches, "Grace to you and peace." Paul used a Greek word for grace and the Hebrew word "shalom" for peace. He probably did so deliberately to connote that both Jews and Gentiles were welcome in the Church.

The seven spirits before the throne could refer to the seven angels provided for each of the seven churches, described at the end of Chapter 1, or this may refer simply to the Holy Spirit, complete and available to every church.

Jesus is proclaimed to be Christ who by way of elaboration is also referred to as "the faithful witness," "the firstborn of the dead," and "the ruler of the kings of the earth." These will become primary themes of the book.

- As "Christ," Jesus is not simply given a name; this is a statement of his office and attainment as the triumphant messiah.

- As "faithful witness," Jesus once stood before Pilate, a Roman authority, and bore testimony at the cost of his life.
- As "firstborn from the dead," he assures those to be martyred in the persecution that they have a future beyond death. The resurrection of Jesus was more than an isolated event; it was their assurance of a future life with God.

Note that because Christ loved us, he "freed us from our sins by his blood." The people of Israel believed that life was in the blood.[11] The blood of animals on the altar was accepted by God as atonement for sin and a substitute for the blood of the people who committed the sin. Christians were oppressed at that time, but it is important to realize that the oppressed are also sinners in need of atonement, like the oppressors. As Christians who have received this atonement, however, they are freed from the consequences of their sin.

We are almost overwhelmed with awe as we realize that we, like those first-century Christians, have been made a "kingdom of priests." Israel had been designated by God as such a kingdom.[12] Christ has now anointed us as priests. Perhaps the Church today should ordain each member as a priest, to help drive home the truth that we have been made "...a kingdom, priests serving his God and Father...." (1:6)

---

[11] Leviticus 17:10-11

[12] Exodus 19:6

The "Amen" at the end of this doxology is the same one we use to close our prayers. It is the Hebrew word meaning "So be it," or "May it happen this way."

"I, John, your brother...." John does not need an official title. He is part of the community of his readers. He has been imprisoned on the isle of Patmos for his preaching and teaching. He writes to "seven churches." In the next two chapters he will pen specific short letters to each of them. There were many more than seven churches in Asia Minor in southwest Turkey. Most of them were established by Paul about 50 A.D. The number seven is a symbol for the complete working out of God's plan, so in a larger sense John writes to all the churches, even to ours today.

"Look" is like a trumpet call, designed to rivet our attention. "He is coming with the clouds" is the vision of Christ in glory.[13] "Every eye will see him" emphasizes the universality of humanity's fulfillment in Christ. "Even those who pierced him" further emphasizes that everyone, including those who pierced Jesus' side with the sword at Calvary, [14] will see the truth.[15]

In verse eight God is declared to be "the Alpha and the Omega." Alpha is the "A" in the Greek alphabet and Omega is the "Z," the first and last letters,

---

13 Matthew 24:30

14 Zechariah 12:10

15 John 19:34

the beginning and the end. God has always existed, exists now, and will always exist.

John Connects with the Churches (Revelation 1:9-11)

In verse nine John says he shares in the persecution, but more importantly, he shares in the kingdom. In the days ahead the entire Church will need to share "patient endurance."

John was on the island of Patmos. Patmos is an island in the Aegean Sea, often designated as the eastern Mediterranean, some 75 miles from Ephesus. It is 10 miles long and six miles wide. The island is volcanic, bare and rocky. It had a town and a school, but it also had a penal colony designed for persons who were viewed as trouble makers for the Romans. Caesar's agents imprisoned John because he preached the truth as revealed by Jesus.

John was "in the Spirit on the Lord's Day." "In the Spirit" means that John was in a state of inspiration that allowed him access to the visions he was about to describe. This "on the Lord's Day" is the first known use of this term to refer to the day of Christian worship. We know the Church assembled on the first day of the week.[16] The day of worship was changed because the first day of the week was the day of the Resurrection. Changing from Saturday may also have been done to distinguish the Christians from the Jews. While John's

---

[16] Acts 20:7; 1 Corinthians 16:2

flock was worshipping in their congregations on the Lord's Day, he was alone. He must have felt their presence as he was "in the Spirit." Note that the coming vision is not one John sought. It sought him.

The Introductory Vision (Revelation 1:12-16)

"I saw seven golden lampstands." The Jewish people always used a seven branched candelabrum on their altars—as God instructed Moses on Mount Sinai after giving the Ten Commandments—to symbolize the perfect outworking of God's plan for His people.[17] The seven lampstands, we learn, represent the seven churches. The vision is that of Christ among the churches John knows and loves. The details are chosen carefully, using the language and images of Old Testament scripture, especially Daniel, chapters seven and ten.

First, the one in their midst wears a long white robe, as worn by a priest. He also wears a golden sash, the kind worn by a king.[18] The one who stands in the midst of the churches is both a priest and a king. He has dazzling white hair; he has the wisdom of the ancients.[19] His eyes are like a flame of fire. The prophet Daniel saw one whose eyes were like flaming torches;[20] he has piercing insight. His feet are like

---

[17] Exodus 25:31-37

[18] 1 Macabees 10:89

[19] Daniel 7:9

[20] Daniel 10:6

burnished bronze; he walks where he will. His voice is like the sound of waves crashing against the shore. In Daniel these were the attributes of a heavenly messenger.[21]

Next is the description of the seven stars held in his right hand. Stars are the cosmic symbol for destiny; here is the cosmic magnitude of the Church's Lord. In the end, events in the world are not shaped by blind fate or by the stars or by human initiative, but rather they unfold according to the plan of God revealed in Christ.

"From his mouth issues a sharp two-edged sword." Hebrews 4:12 says, "The word of the Lord is living and active, sharper than any two-edged sword…able to discern reflections and thoughts of the heart."

"His face was like the sun shining in full strength." This is the same Lord who was once transfigured on the mountain with his select disciples.

The Vision Explained (Revelation 1:17-20)

John said that when he saw this Christ he fell at his feet as though dead. His reaction was similar to others in the Bible suddenly confronted by the Almighty.[22] But the risen Lord told John not to be afraid. He is alive forever and he now has authority over death.

---

[21] Daniel 6:13

[22] Daniel 8:17; Acts 26:14

Then he explained to John the meaning of the seven stars and the seven golden lampstands. The seven stars are angels of the seven churches, and the seven lampstands are the seven churches. Now let us review the vision so that its impact may strike us fully.

Stamp indelibly on your mind the picture of Christ among the lampstands. His presence makes the Church a divine institution. Apart from Christ it is a mere human organization. He is always present, despite efforts by powerful people to destroy the churches and the gullibility of some members who are deluded by false prophets. Look with me again at the description of Christ.

Christ wears the robe of a high priest. He is girded with the sash of a king. His hair is white as wool; he is as old as eternity. His eyes are as a flame of fire. Christ searches the heart and sees all things. His feet are like burnished bronze refined in fire. The Savior can walk where he wills. His voice is like mighty waters; He speaks with authority. A sharp two-edged sword issues from his mouth. His words pierce the heart and judge our sins.

Do you get the full impact of this vision? The divine Christ, our high priest, king over kings of earth, who existed before all time, who knows all about us, who has all power and authority, who judges the good and the bad, and who speaks the words of eternal life—this Christ stands in the midst of the churches and holds their eternal destiny in his hand. His presence, his power, and his guidance are the divine guarantee of the Church's ultimate triumph!

Our Guarantee Also

This is the message of Revelation, and it is as relevant for us as for those to whom it was written. Those small struggling congregations seemed destined for extinction. How could they stand against the edict of the Roman Emperor? This vision of victory helped the Christians not just to endure, but even to triumph! It can do the same for us.

A Postscript

There is historical evidence that Paul, who founded these churches forty years earlier, was finally beheaded as a Christian martyr.

In imagination I hear the ring of the headsman's ax and then we join Paul as he approaches the portals of heaven. What about the churches? Can they survive? How can they stand against the edict of the world's most powerful ruler? In my imagination I now see the doors of heaven open. I visualize angels rushing forward to welcome and congratulate Paul. But the old Apostle's mind is troubled. Even in glory he cannot rejoice. He pushes his way past the heavenly hosts to look through the windows of heaven to the earth below. What about the churches? Will they survive? Will the Christians stand firm in the face of persecution?

Paul then sees the seven golden lampstands. There stands the Savior in the midst of the churches, holding the seven stars in his right hand. Paul's mind is flooded with relief at the realization that Christ is leading the churches and their eternal destiny is secure. Only then does he shout his triumphant "Hallelujah!"

Questions for Reflection

1. Does it matter if the John who wrote Revelation was not John, the disciple of Jesus?
2. Do you begin to see how the imagery is taken from Hebrew scripture?
3. Do we dare agree with John's vision of Christ present in the churches? Can the churches be destroyed? Can they be destroyed only by our unfaithful witness?
4. Should the church ordain every new member as a priest? Why or why not?
5. Note none is a "priestess." "Kingdom" connotes a "king" or male ruler. All of the language is masculine. Is this because the book was the product of a male culture? Is it because all rule and authority is inherently ordained by God to come through men only? Or, is this simply a literary device, where use of the male implies both male and female?

Chapter 3

FAITHFUL UNTIL DEATH
Revelation 2, 3

> Be faithful until death, and I will give you the crown of life.
>
> —Revelation 2:10b

Before examining John's letters to each of seven churches it may be helpful to look at a road map to learn where we are going. The writer has three purposes. Quite simply, he wants to state a fact, present a challenge, and offer a promise.

The Fact

First, God rules the world. This fact is expressed again and again. A depraved ruler sits at the controls of the empire. But God waits in the shadows, keeping watch over His own. To the casual observer it appears that the powers of darkness are harnessed and riding to victory, but a closer look shows that God holds the reins. God is using people and events to accomplish His purpose, despite wicked persons who have no desire to serve him.

The Roman government hoped to discredit and even destroy the churches through persecution of its members. Instead the tribulation purified and strengthened them. Those who loved earthly life more than Christ were cast aside, while the sterling character of the saints became more pure and radiant. As at Calvary, God used evil deeds for His glory.

The Challenge

John's second purpose is to present a challenge. His fellow church members are challenged to remain faithful unto death. Many of the symbolic pictures in Revelation show that this suffering may be long and hard. They encounter a dragon, powerful evil beasts and a woman dressed in scarlet bent on their destruction. Satan, the Roman Empire, the Council to enforce emperor worship, and the city of Rome will all conspire against them.

The remains of the Coliseum still stand in Rome. Here in the arena our sisters and brothers in Christ were torn to pieces by lions for the amusement of the crowds. In the remains of the Coliseum today you can see the narrow steps that the Christians climbed to meet their death. These steps are hallowed by the blood of faithful witnesses.

In an earlier decade, during the reign of Nero, the Christians had learned what it meant to be hunted and killed for their faith. "They were put to death with exquisite cruelty," said Tacitus, a Roman historian, "and to their suffering Nero added mockery and derision. Some were covered with the skins of wild beasts and left to be devoured by dogs; others were nailed to crosses; numbers were burned alive; and many, covered with inflammable matter, were lighted up when the day declined to serve as torches during the night."

The challenge is to be faithful until death.

The Promise

John's third purpose is to offer a promise, "I will give you the crown of life." Regardless of what happens to us on earth, there is a home and a crown for those who are faithful to Christ. This promised life is everlasting and abundant. Every possible symbol of rich fulfillment is employed to help the saints realize the glory that lies ahead. Even in the present, this vision can attune us to the strength and inspiration available through a conscious connection with Christ and our heavenly counterparts. One can press on with such a prize.

There will be victory not only because Christ is the leader, but also because of the support of the invisible Church in heaven. As the drama unfolds, the earthly scene is interrupted many times to encourage the faltering Christians. Heaven's door opens wide enough for them to see the support they have there. These heavenly hosts eagerly watch the happenings on earth. They extend their love and compassion to those in tribulation. The churches gain strength by knowing they are "outposts of a heavenly fellowship."

Now we turn to the text to examine John's letters to the seven churches. There are certain basic elements in each letter. First, Christ is identified as the divine author, using words taken from the description of Christ among the churches in Chapter 1. Next is an assertion that Christ knows all about the particular church, with its strengths and weaknesses. There follows a recognition of problems related to the persecution. Finally, there is the promise of divine help. These elements are present in each of the letters to the seven churches.

The Church at Ephesus (Revelation 2:1-7)

Ephesus was a splendid metropolis that boasted a busy seaport. The seat of government had been moved to the rival city of Pergamum, but Ephesus was still the center for commercial and cultural activities. At the time of this letter, the church at Ephesus may have been the most important Christian church in the Roman Empire. It was the headquarters for Paul's missionary strategy and had become the mother church of the region. Paul's first visit is described in Acts 18:19-21, and his return stay of three years is recorded in Acts 19-20.

The city had long promoted emperor worship. As early as 29 A.D., Augustus Caesar persuaded the city to build and dedicate a temple to Julius Caesar. When persecution of Christians had not yet become widespread elsewhere, feelings ran high against followers of Christ here. This church was described in early Christian literature as "the road of the martyrs."

The letter begins with encouragement. "I know your works, your toil and your patient endurance." Toil in this setting refers to their struggle to maintain their Christian faith and practice in the face of adversity. He was saying, "I know the going is hard." Patient endurance is a high virtue in Revelation; repeatedly Christians are urged simply to endure.

"But I have this against you, that you have abandoned the love you had at first." When Paul left Ephesus the people were ready to do anything for Christ. No demand was too great. They were riding the wave of enthusiastic devotion. By the time of this letter they were second and third generation Christians. The people began to coast. Paul had warned them not to become weary in well-doing, but there was a letdown. Listen to these words, "Remember then from what you have fallen; repent, and do the works you did at first."

The church is praised for testing false prophets. Visiting preachers and self-proclaimed prophets are not all authentic witnesses. Some were hucksters interested in personal gain; others were sincere advocates of heresies that, nonetheless, weakened the integrity and power of the gospel.

John warned against the Nicolaitans. They were Gnostics, followers of a form of Greek philosophy which taught that Christians could not be hurt spiritually by sinning, since they had been redeemed. They ate meat offered to idols and some joined in sexual orgies at idolatrous feasts. Such advocates of license must be isolated and removed from the body of Christ.

The letter ends with John's plea to the Christians at Ephesus to pay attention to his letter and a promise that they will be rewarded for their faithfulness.

The Church at Smyrna (Revelation 2:8-11)

Smyrna was a progressive seaport city with a large Jewish population. The city still exists as Ixmir; it has had a Christian community for well over 1,900 years. Located 35 miles north of Ephesus, it was a beautiful resort city and was known as "the fairest city of all the cities."

But all was not well there for the Christian community. Some Jewish leaders had turned against the Christians when converts left Judaism. These leaders devised ways to make Christians look bad in the eyes of Roman authorities. Christians were brought into court on some pretense and then had their property confiscated because they would not say, "Caesar is Lord." Many times they lost their livelihoods as well. John says, "I know your affliction and your poverty, even though you are rich." Paul, too, had experienced their plight and had written, "...having nothing, and yet possessing everything." (2 Corinthians 6:10)

Then came a warning. Some of them would be thrown into prison for ten days. Ten is the symbol for completeness. Christians would be persecuted until the wrath of the Romans and Jews exhausted itself. They were then offered the challenge and promise discussed at the beginning of this chapter: "Be faithful until death, and I will give you the crown of life."

Smyrna was famous for its bloody games. Thousands of spectators came to the large arena to witness the fights. They watched as gladiators faced each other in duels to the death. The crowds cheered wildly when the winner was presented a crown as a reward for victory.

John said that in like manner the Church was in a duel with the Roman Empire. The Christians were not asked to win the contest in their own strength; they were asked to remain faithful until death. God would award the crown—a crown of everlasting life.

There is an historical account of the death of Polycarp, the bishop of Smyrna in this arena in 155 A.D. Polycarp was commanded to put incense on the altar to Caesar and say, "Caesar is Lord." Polycarp had refused and was then brought to the arena. The crowds gathered. The governor from his box in the stands shouted, "Swear by Caesar."

Polycarp replied, "I am a Christian. I swear only by Christ."

"I'll have you thrown to the beasts," came back the governor's angry threat.

"Bring on the beasts," shouted Polycarp.

"If you scorn the beasts, I'll have you burned."

"You are trying to frighten me with the fire that burns for an hour, and you forget the fire of hell that never goes out!"

As the flames leapt high that day in the arena, Polycarp's final prayer was, "Lord God Almighty, Father of our Lord Jesus Christ, I bless Thee that Thou deemed me worthy of this hour.... May I be an acceptable sacrifice...through Jesus Christ."

As Polycarp died he must have had in his mind the words written to his church, "Be faithful until death, and I will give you the crown of life."

The Church at Pergamum (Revelation 2:12-17)

Pergamum was the administrative headquarters for Asia Minor, located forty miles north of Smyrna. This church, we learn, was located in the stronghold of Satan. The city was a religious center with temples to many gods including three temples dedicated to three different Caesars. A great altar to Zeus, chief of the gods, had been erected high on the Acropolis overlooking the city. Part of his altar remains to this day and is on display at the Pergamum museum in Berlin. Pergamum was aggressively pagan and openly opposed to Christianity. The regional court there had as its official emblem "the sword of justice." To this church Christ was identified as one who has the sharp two-edged sword.

The chief concern of John was that some of those same Nicolaitans, Gnostic heretics who had been rebuffed at Ephesus, had been accepted into the church in Pergamum. They ate meat offered to idols, condoned sexual immorality at the pagan feasts they attended, and reasoned that since they were led by the Holy Spirit, these practices could do them no harm. This attitude was a dangerous perversion of Christianity.

The martyr Antipas is remembered with appreciation. Notice that most people in this church were faithful. Only a few followed false teachers.

Christ would make war with his two-edged sword against the offenders, not the entire church. Yet the congregation is chastised for failing to take vigorous steps to stamp out the false teaching.

Those who conquer are given hidden manna and a white stone with a name written on it. What does this mean? The people were aware of a legend that Jeremiah hid the "ark of the covenant" in a cave and it contained a jar of the manna kept from the time the Israelites had wandered in the wilderness. When Israel was truly free, the legend said, they would feast on this manna. The white amulet inscribed with a name refers to an ancient pagan practice of taking a white stone, writing the name of a god on it, and using it as a charm for protection. Here Christians will figuratively write the name of Christ on their own white amulet.

The Church at Thyatira (Revelation 2:18-28)

Thyatira was located in a broad valley forty miles southeast of Pergamum. It was primarily a trading and manufacturing center with its trade guilds. The issue, again, was the extent to which the Christians were tempted to conform to the prevailing culture.

The Spirit sees through appearances, with eyes that flash like fire. All of the sins in this church are quickly detected. But first there is praise. They grew in grace; they made progress in spiritual living. But they tolerated an evil woman in the church who styled herself a prophetess but was really a spiritual descendant of Jezebel. Bible scholars will recall that Jezebel was the pagan wife of King Ahab of Israel. She had been determined to introduce her pagan idols to her husband's people.[23]

This congregation also fell prey to the heretical belief that one cannot sin so long as she or he is under grace. These Gnostic teachers claimed to have understanding "into the deep things of God." John placed words in the mouth of Jesus saying their understanding is rather of "the deep things of Satan."

Before becoming too critical of these parishioners, we should realize how difficult it was to be a Christian in a pagan society. The pressure to place incense on the altar in worship of the emperor was only one of many related problems. Plays at the theater were built around stories of the gods, or they were coarse and immoral. Sports in the arena were bloody and inhumane. Textbooks in the schools centered on the exploits of pagan gods. The sculptor who chiseled tombstones for a living was forced to engrave the images of gods on them or he would find no buyers. To go to court meant to swear by the gods. Most of the skilled workers belonged to trade guilds. Each guild had its own god. One does not appreciate the unconscious influences of Christianity on our society until we look back on an era where Christianity was a foreign element.

"...To the one who conquers I will also give the morning star." (2:28) Out of the midnight of struggle

---

[23] 1 Kings 16:31-33

will come the sunburst of the morning for those who are determined to live within the will of God.

The Church at Sardis (Revelation 3:1-6)

Sardis was a city set on a hill, about thirty miles southeast of Thyatira. There was a high cliff around three sides of the city. Only through a narrow strip on the south side could an invader penetrate the stronghold. Despite this protection, the city had been destroyed twice when troops poured in through this unprotected narrow crevice in the rock. Rome levied no tax on Sardis for five years so the city would have money to rebuild.

The church at Sardis was widely renowned. There was splendor in her worship. She sought her members from among the well-to-do, but forgot humility and lowly deeds of sacrificial service. She was a church that had good public relations with the world but a deaf ear to the voice of God.

"You have the name of being alive but you are dead." This church received more criticism than any of the others. The church had been spared persecution and false teachers. While the external image was of a successful church, the gaze of the Lord went deeper.

Fortunately, there is opportunity for these lukewarm Christians to repent. A minority of members are commended for faithfulness. They were the spark at Sardis that kept the spiritual life from going out entirely. We are told their names will not be blotted out of the book of life. In Sardis each citizen had his name inscribed in a book of tax records. Those whose names were in the book were considered to be citizens; those not in the book were aliens. Symbolically, the same kind of book is kept in heaven.

The Church at Philadelphia (Revelation 3:7-14)

Philadelphia was a small city twenty-five miles southeast of Sardis. The congregation was small and mostly from the lower class. It was subject to severe pressure from a strong Jewish population. In some respects it was similar to the church in Smyrna. Like its sister church, this one received only praise. The struggling church got what it needed most—encouragement. "I know your works," says the Lord, "...you have but little power, and yet you have kept my word and have not denied my name.... Because you have kept my word of patient endurance, I will keep you from the hour of trial that is coming on the whole world to test the inhabitants of the earth."

In 17 A.D., Philadelphia had experienced an earthquake of unprecedented proportions. Buildings were destroyed. Seventy-five years later buildings again trembled. The angel said to this church, "I will make you a pillar in the temple of my God; you will never go out of it." Their numbers were small but their witness was sure.

The Church at Laodicea (Revelation 3:14-23)

Finally, there was the church at Laodicea, located forty miles southeast of Philadelphia. This church was neither hot nor cold. John wished they were one or the other, for Christ could not use them when they were lukewarm. They said they were rich, prosperous, and in need of nothing. Actually, they were "wretched, pitiable, poor, blind, and naked." If they had been cold, they might have felt the need for spiritual clothing. But in their self-satisfied state they never perceived their weakness. This church suffered the greatest condemnation. God is sick of mere form, sham and outward parade. They are counseled to "buy from me gold refined by fire so that you may be rich."

Outside the city of Laodicea were the hot springs of Hieropolos. Water flowed through an aqueduct from the springs into the city but by the time it got there it had cooled and was lukewarm. Lukewarm commitment is inadequate for the Christian community.[24]

The city of Laodicea was famous in three ways. It was recognized throughout the ancient world as a great banking center. Laodicea was also the center of an important sheep-raising region where black, glossy wool was woven into famous patterns of cloth. Third, Laodicea was a noted medical center. The city still has coins showing the medical rod and serpent. It was made famous by an ointment for eye disease. In this center of banking, cloth making, and eye treatment, John called the church "poor, naked and blind."

---

[24] Chapman, Charles E., *The Message of the Book of Revelation* (The Liturgical Press: Collegeville, MN, p. 36)

Despite the severe rebuke, John did not want to leave the members feeling utterly hopeless. Criticism was tempered with compassion and a deep desire to see them repent. Jesus said to them, "Listen, I am standing at the door, knocking; if you hear my voice and open the door, I will come in to you and eat with you, and you with me." To eat a feast with a king was an ancient symbol of bliss. This golden opportunity is still available to every dormant church that opens the door and lets Christ come in.

Postscript

I went to Saint Paul's Cathedral in London and viewed that magnificent painting "The Light of the World" by Holman Hunt (1827-1910). In the painting Christ stands at the door and knocks. A crown of thorns is on his head as a symbol of self-sacrifice. The door is the soul of a person. That door is barred. Its bars are rusty, and around the door creeping tendrils of ivy show that it has been shut for a long time. Christ comes in the night. He is alone. He does not come to discredit but rather to encounter each of us privately and personally. He is wearing the white robe, symbol of purity. He has a jeweled breastplate, indicating the richness of his life. And if you look closely, you see a crown of gold interlaced with the crown of thorns. Any person who opens the door of her or his heart and permits Christ to come in will receive abundant blessings.

I watched people pass the painting as if they did not see it. They glanced up and went on. I was saddened. Here was a world famous painting, a magnificent portrait of Christ asking admittance into our lives, and people casually passed by. That, too, has a meaning. People of the Roman world looked with contempt at a meek Savior bringing salvation. People of today pass the Christ without a second glance. But our broken world will be mended as we hear that knock and open the door. Our churches will be luke-warm and unconcerned until we open the door where Christ stands waiting.

Questions for Reflection and Discussion

1. John saw two dangers facing the church: persecution and inward decay. Do you know churches that have the outward appearance of success but that are spiritually quite dead?

2. Should our churches attempt to discipline members for heresy or for lax behavior? What are the benefits and the dangers? How could a church serious about its spiritual life deal with these issues?

3. John wrote to the church at Ephesus to admonish them about waning commitment. John told us also what to do under these circumstances: "Remember...repent...do the works." Comment.

4. "America has a Christian culture." In what sense is this statement true? In what sense false? How should we accommodate persons of other religions or no religion at all?

Chapter 4

GOD ON THE THRONE
Revelation 4, 5

Holy, holy, holy, all the saints adore Thee,
Casting down their golden crowns
Around the glassy sea.
Cherubim and Seraphim falling down before Thee
Which wert, and art, and ever more shall be.[25]

The persecuted Christians at the close of the New Testament era felt safe only if they were sure of God's protective care. Could they be torn away from the Omnipotent, Omnipresent God? Could they stand in the face of persecution? In order to endure they needed a clear picture of Almighty God reigning from the throne in heaven.

Here is the heart of the book of Revelation. More important than predicting future events is an understanding of what lies behind those events. God is on the throne, ruling, caring, loving and working out the divine plan for humanity.

---

[25] Hymn "Holy, Holy, Holy" by Reginald Heber (1783-1826)

Seeing through Heaven's Door

At the beginning of Chapter 4, John turns his attention from the persecuted churches of Asia and looks up through an open door into heaven itself. His theological purpose is to help his readers learn who is Lord of the world. Is it Caesar? Or is it Christ?

A voice like a trumpet invites him to watch. He is summoned by an angel, identical to the one who introduced the first vision in Chapter 1. John is awestruck as his eyes focus on the eternal throne of God. Of course, he is not able to see or describe God. All he can see is the heavenly radiance surrounding God. What John describes is a splendor that he compares to various jewels. The jasper is a bright shining stone; the carnelian is a bright red, transparent stone. The other color is green that turns to blue, like the shining of an emerald. John discerns a rainbow around God, a symbol of living hope (4:3).

In front of the throne is "a sea of glass, like crystal" that keeps the believer a proper distance from God. Some day the sea will be no more, and Christians will stand in the near presence of God. Now, however, the sea serves as a gulf between frail humanity and omnipotent sovereignty. The sea symbolizes the truth spoken by the prophet Isaiah: "For as the heavens are higher than the earth, so are my ways higher than your ways and my thoughts than your thoughts."[26]

---

[26] Isaiah 55:9

John sees twenty-four thrones on which sit twenty-four elders. They wear white robes and golden crowns. Most scholars believe the twenty-four elders represent the twelve sons of Jacob who became the twelve tribes of Israel, and the other twelve represent the twelve inner disciples of Christ. Twelve is the symbol of organized religion; twenty-four is twelve doubled. The golden crowns cast before the throne is a reference to a contemporary court ceremony in which local leaders or lesser kings expressed their allegiance to a greater ruler. For example, when Nero was crowned as Roman Emperor, according to the Roman writer, Tacitus, the Parthian King Tiridates placed his diadem or crown before the image of Nero in homage to the Roman Emperor.

The lightening, thunder and voices are all based on Old Testament experiences.[27] They make the senses aware of the might and mystery of God. The seven torches that burn before the throne remind us of the lampstand in the holy of holies of the Jerusalem Temple (4:5).

Around God are four living creatures full of eyes and with six wings. This vision is taken from the experience of Isaiah when he saw God in the temple and accepted the call to be a prophet.[28] Also, Zechariah, the prophet, had said, "The eyes of the Lord range over the

---

[27] Ezekiel 1:13, 14; Job 37:4-5

[28] Isaiah 6

whole earth."[29] The eyes are a symbol of God's omniscience; God sees and knows everything.

God, the Creator

As John listened enraptured, he heard the twenty-four elders join the living creatures in a song of praise to God for His creation.[30] Here is heavenly worship that never ends. The creatures sing and the elders respond. "You are worthy" are the words shouted by the crowds at the inauguration of Domitian. The very act of shouting these words by the throng imparted power to the ruler.

"You are worthy, our Lord and God, to receive glory and honor and power, for you created all things, and by your will they existed and were created." (4:11)

Christ, the Redeemer

As John continued to watch, he saw those before the throne bow in intense reverence to the Lamb that was slain. The image of the lion-like lamb occurs 28 times in Revelation and always signifies the resurrected Christ. All the living creatures fell before Christ and sang a new song: "You are worthy to take the scroll and to open its seals, for you were slaughtered and by your blood you ransomed for God saints from every tribe and language and people and nation…." (5:9) When God on the throne handed Jesus, the Lamb, the sealed scroll, it was a sign that he shared equally with God. When a

---

[29] Zechariah 4:10

[30] Genesis 1:1

King sealed a scroll and dispatched it, only the person for whom it was intended could break the seal and open the scroll. Christ was the only one in heaven worthy to open the scroll.

Note that Christ received the same joyous adoration and praise as did God. It was he who paid the price for sin by his own suffering. It was Christ who ransomed men for God regardless of their origin or language.

The ransom paid by Christ was not blackmail exacted by Satan. Neither was it an appeasement paid to any angry ruler. It was not a payment TO anyone. Rather, it was a payment FOR you and me. It is intended to say that Jesus, through giving up his life, emancipated people from the power of sin and made it possible for them to live in the immense grace of God's presence.

Note again the exciting, wonderful universal salvation. "You are worthy to take the scroll and to open its seals, for you were slaughtered and by your blood you ransomed for God saints from every tribe and language and people and nation; you have made them to be a kingdom and priests serving our God, and they will reign on earth." (5:9-10)

This thrilling vision of the end-time community reveals how people who belong to God will rule as priests to God.[31] This community is destined for rule over the renewed earth (20:6). John insists that final

---

[31] 1 Timothy 6:15-16

redemption does not pertain just to individuals but requires the whole world to be free from oppression.

The heavenly liturgy is expanded even further. In Daniel[32] we read of the endless expansion of praise through the expression of 10,000 times 10,000 new voices that join in the praise—an incalculable throng.

So John sees that the saving work of the Lamb belongs together with God's work of creation. His salvation extends to all regions of the world and all periods of history, grounded in Jesus' historical work of teaching the kingdom of God.

A Postscript on Worship

Chapter 5 closes with the words, "And the four living creatures said, 'Amen!' And the elders fell down and worshiped." (5:14)

This I Believe

Here is a panorama of worship unequaled elsewhere in Holy Writ. In the presence of this overwhelming experience of adoration and praise, I pause to ponder the meaning of our worship.

First, worship is our response to the majesty of God. The crystal sea around the throne says symbolically that God is above and beyond us. Mystery cloaks God. The One on the throne is not the maid who cleans our spiritual houses. This is not Santa Claus minus the red suit. God is not the quarterback on

---

[32] Daniel 7:10

our team whose clever calling of plays helps us win the game of life. God is not "the old man upstairs." Rather, as Paul wrote to Timothy, God is "…the blessed and only Sovereign, the King of kings and Lord of lords. It is he alone who has immortality and dwells in unapproachable light, whom no one has ever seen or can see…."[33]

God's majesty is so great, the psalmist with all of his imagination and feeling could not begin to describe the wonder. "The heavens are telling the glory of God; and the firmament proclaims his handiwork. Day to day pours forth speech, and night to night declares knowledge."[34] How much greater God is than the blazing sun or host of twinkling stars that are the creation of His hand!

Second, worship is our response to the judgment of God. Speaking poetically, we come each day into the court of the universe. God sits on the judge's bench; we are on the witness stand. There is no mistake when the verdict is announced. It is this supreme judge who made right and wrong. When we break God's law, we are guilty. God's piercing eye of fire burns into our souls and scrutinizes our sins. "Coming from the throne are flashes of lightning, and rumblings and peals of thunder…." (4:5) The living creatures who sing before the throne say, "Holy, holy, holy, the Lord God, the Almighty."

---

[33] 1 Timothy 6:15-16

[34] Psalm 19:1-2

To wink at sin would be for God to say that right and wrong are not important. If we could break the laws of the state without trial or punishment, there would be little respect for right conduct. If we could defy God, wayward humanity would never come into right relationship with either God or other persons. God is a holy God. Worship is our response to the righteous God who judges our sin.

The third aspect of worship is our response to God's love for us. Christ died for our sins. God loved the world so much that, being present with Jesus on the cross, God's heart was also pierced, as with a spear. Our worship is the acceptance of this magnificent love. Here is love that gives, yearns, searches, forgives and dies for us. At the center of God's nature is this heart throb of love for us. Here, I believe, is the deepest truth of the universe.

What is worship? See the justice of God and we want to run like the psalmist who said, "Where can I go from your Spirit? Or where can I flee from your presence?" [35] Perhaps I try to escape, but without success. As Philo of Alexandria, the great Jewish philosopher, (20 B.C. to 50 A.D.) observed, "Just try to flee from water or air, from the sky or from the whole of the world.... If we cannot hide from the world...how can we hide from God?"

But in that moment of fear and self-humiliation, I hear the call of His love and mercy reaching down to

---

[35] Psalm 139:7

me. I am drawn by an irresistible attraction. "And I, when I am lifted up from the earth, will draw all people to myself."[36] I cry out, "My soul longs, indeed it faints for the courts of the Lord; my heart and my flesh sing for joy to the living God."[37]

Worship is the recognition of the majesty of God as our creator, the holiness of God as our judge, and the compassion of God as our redeemer.

The Power of This Vision

Martin Luther penned one of our great hymns of worship, "A Mighty Fortress Is Our God." In a dark age Luther gave hope to Europe and set people to singing the gospel. Carlyle wrote of this hymn, "There is something in it like the sound of Alpine avalanches or the first murmur of earthquakes." Luther experienced as much as any person "the flood of mortal ills prevailing," yet his "mighty fortress" was God.

This same overwhelming conviction of strength flooded the thoughts of those early Christians. Broken were the shackles of dread. Fear gave way to faith through John's vision of God who created and controlled all things. As with Luther those early Christians said, "The right Man is on our side, the Man of God's own choosing.... And he must win the battle."

---

[36] John 12:32

[37] Psalm 84:2

The God of our day is the same God who sat on the throne when John looked beyond heaven's door. Our high privilege is to trust as did those early Christian martyrs. We can join every creature in heaven and on earth and under the earth and in the sea and say with them, "To him who sits upon the throne and to the Lamb be blessing and honor and glory and might forever and ever! ...Amen...." (5:13-14)

Questions for Discussion

1. The traditional formulation of the Godhead is: God the Father, the Son, and the Holy Spirit. With great effort I have avoided this formulation here, because John does not use it. Note in these chapters how God and Jesus are named. Why?
2. Do you hold a vision of a redeemed social order as well as redeemed individuals?
3. Comment on my presentation of worship.
4. What do you see as the relationship between justice and love?
5. If God cares for all persons equally, can God condone injustice of one person or group toward another? Does not this call for the wrath of God?
6. A father was asked how he would react if his son were found to have committed a crime. He said, "I forgive him before he ever does the evil deed." Does this not fail to deal with evil and its consequence for the innocent? Should the son be forgiven before he has dealt with his crime?

Chapter 5

THE RIDE OF THE FOUR HORSEMEN
and
SIX SEALS OPENED
Revelation 6, 7

The Roman Empire was like a great mowing machine bearing down on the early Christians. The book of Revelation was written to believers who felt they had little chance of survival. They were being cut down by forces beyond their control. The Empire was too powerful for them. They seemed weak and isolated. But were they really helpless? To answer that question we now study the opening of six of seven seals and see what God has to say. (The opening of the seventh seal comes later.)

In the ancient Mediterranean world the king, when waging war, would write out a plan of battle on a scroll and then seal it with wax. He would entrust the scroll to a messenger who would deliver it to his military general. Any unauthorized person who broke the seal and read the message would be put to death.

In Chapter 5 we read there was weeping in heaven and earth because nobody was deemed worthy to open the seals to prepare for battle. But then we are told, "Do not weep. See, the Lion of the tribe of Judah, the Root of David, has conquered, so that he can open the scroll and its seven seals." (5:5) Christ will reveal God's plan for the battle that looms ahead.

The Opening of the First Four Seals (Revelation 6:1-8)

"Then I saw the Lamb open one of the seven seals, and I heard one of the four living creatures call out, as with a voice of thunder, 'Come!'" (6:1) Come, take your seat at the stage of world history and get ready for what God has to say. Come and witness a divine revelation!

With that cry, "Come!" the first of four horsemen gallops onto the stage.[38] He rides a white horse. The rider is Christ. The white horse represents the gospel in its purity. The text, I believe, supports this interpretation, although some see the white horse as a symbol of military conquest.[39] The European commentator Jurgen Roloff[40] takes the position that the white horse represents victory in battle and hence this is an evil rider who joins the upcoming three other personifications of evil. M. Eugene Boring[41] agrees, arguing that this is a reference to warriors from Parthis

---

[38] The imagery of the four horsemen is taken from Zechariah 6.

[39] I follow the view of Donald Richardson, *The Revelation of Jesus Christ* (Richmond: John Knox Press, 1939)

[40] Roloff, Jurgen, *Revelation, A Continental Commentary* (trans. John Alsup) (Minneapolis: Fortress Press,1993, p.86)

[41] Boring, M. Eugene, ***op. cit.***, p. 122

in modern Iraq, on the eastern border of the Roman Empire, who were well known as archers and who rode white horses. My own view remains that the white horseman represents Christ. This is confirmed by the picture of Christ in Revelation 19:11-16. Even as the mighty Parthis warriors won many battles, so Christ is the greatest of warriors.

"Its rider had a bow." He rides forth to wage war against unrighteousness. Jesus said, "Do not think that I have come to bring peace to the earth; I have not come to bring peace, but a sword."[42] There can be no alliance with sin. Christ wages a relentless, never-ending war against the other horsemen. "...A crown was given to him, and he came out conquering and to conquer." (6:2) The crown is a reward for victory. Christ will win the coming struggle. He is conquering now; ultimately, He will conquer completely. Christ had said to Simon Peter, "...I will build my church, and the gates of Hades will not prevail against it."[43]

Against whom does the rider of the white horse wage war? Three other horsemen charge forth in succession. The second horse is red, the color of blood. The third horse is black, symbol of famine and starvation. The fourth horse is pale, the color of a corpse.

---

[42] Matthew 10:34

[43] Matthew 16:18

The Red Horse Named War

The rider of the red horse is given a sword. Men slaughter one another as peace disappears from the earth. The red horse is named War.

From this imagery we learn that Christ abhors war. It is opposed to his nature and purpose for humanity. But some say, "The Bible states there will always be wars and rumors of wars." The response of this vision is, "Yes, but Christ is always going up and down the earth opposing war." Many of Jesus' followers wanted him to usher in the kingdom with the sword. He steadfastly refused. His was a strange teaching. "Love your enemies." Love was his only weapon of conquest. For the first three centuries of its existence, the Church almost without exception opposed Christian participation in war.

Across the centuries Christian ethicists developed the doctrine of "the just war." When the Christian faith was accepted by rulers, they needed guidance as to when it was acceptable for them to lead their nations into war. With civic responsibility, they felt the need to balance the imperative of loving one's enemy with the need to do the greatest good for the greatest number of people. It might be a greater injustice not to fight a war than to wage one.

The unflattering truth is that Christian leaders have often forgotten about this doctrine of the just war when inflamed with the passions of national pride or the potential spoils of conflict. Even when they have applied the doctrine, it has often been rationalized so that the will of the ruler took precedence over the claim of the rider on the white horse. Let it be stated clearly that the way of Christ is not one of violence; the way of this warrior is always the rule of impartial law, negotiation, creative non-violence, and the great power that is unleashed by loving one's enemies. We leave open the question of a justifiable war in extreme and unusual circumstances.

The Black Horse of Famine

The next enemy rides forth on a black horse into combat against Christ (6:6). His name is famine. How do we know? The horseman is carrying a balance, and a voice from among the four living creatures says, "A quart of wheat for a day's pay, and three quarts of barley for a day's pay, but do not damage the olive oil and the wine!" That is an entire day's wages for an unskilled worker.[44] The price of food has increased ten-fold because of the scarcity. At that time in Asia Minor, olive oil and wine were produced abundantly. In the event of war and civil unrest, when imports of grain were cut off, the local population could still count on the local crops. But since grain was the staple food of the poor, a drought was a disaster for them. The poor cannot pay the high price for scarce wheat and barley.

This I Believe

Christ today rides against world hunger and poverty. Global unrest and mass uprisings of the

---

44 Matthew 20:9

world's poverty-stricken people are, in my judgment, led by the rider on the white horse. He rides against the black horse of poverty and famine. Christ rides in the cause of the downtrodden, the half-starved masses of humanity. It behooves the international community of nations, America, and each of us to join this work against hunger and poverty, too, or we face defeat from him who rides on the white horse.

Across America in recent decades churches have heard the cries of desperate poor people for food and have opened soup kitchens to serve them. When they give food and drink to the poor, the hungry and thirsty, they do it as if to Christ. Some churches have also been active politically in seeking to influence legislation that provides food stamps, nutrition programs for pregnant mothers and infants, and other programs sponsored by our government to meet needs of the larger population, not just those who are fortunate enough to be served by a church group. Government represents the community taking action for the benefit of all in recognition of our social contract, expressed in the Constitution, to promote the general welfare. When we work for such legislation we also ride alongside Christ on the white horse in his war against poverty and hunger.

Since Christ's love is for all the people of the world, we can take the logical next step and recognize our responsibility for the billion people of the world who live in what has been called "absolute poverty." These are people with a total annual income of less than $400 per year expressed in our dollars. According to

Global Issues (January 2013) the 40% of the world's poorest people have only 5 percent of global income. And according to UNESCO, 22,000 children die every day due to poverty. Are there specific policies of our nation that work to our advantage against the poor nations?

Specifically, should Christians be concerned about tariff policies, interest rates, International Monetary Fund policies, debt relief to poor nations, exploitation of natural resources along with environmental degradation, and other policies that result in poverty for many and wealth for a few? Can we envision a network of concerned persons interested in justice for all? Can we devise ways to support our common humanity in a plan for greater global justice? Those who call Christ Lord can enter this network of those committed to economic justice, assured that Christ on his white horse rides alongside.[45]

The Ride of Death

A final horseman thunders into view. He rides the pale horse named Death (6:8). War and injustice often result in death. Jesus also came to bring abundant life in the battle against disease. In his earthly ministry he did not say that illness is the will of God. Neither did he imply that we should simply accept our fate. He went everywhere healing the sick.

---

[45] For a fuller discussion of this issue see McCan, Robert, *World Economy and World Hunger* (Washington, D.C.: University Publications of America, 1982).

He was at war against the demons of disease, and he cast them out of sick people. He showed that it is God's will that we live in good health.

It is interesting for us to note that in the midst of his concern about specific problems facing the seven churches, John widens the perspective and writes about other enemies of Christ. Yes, the Lord is relentless in his war against the evils of the empire, representing unjust worldly power at that time, and we are reminded that Christ in his years of ministry also fought against injustice, poverty and illness.

But there is another death beyond physical death. The pale horse brings spiritual death also. Satan is depicted as riding behind death, eager to reach out and snatch each victim. The greater tragedy is to deny the call of Christ and to ignore the signs God gives us that show us our need to repent and live with vitality. The tragedy is to have our souls sink into the abyss of self-centered delusion. Christ on the white horse of the gospel will also defeat this final enemy of humanity.

The Cry of the Martyrs

With the opening of the fifth seal, the scene narrows and intensifies. It is not so much that the scene shifts to heaven as it is that events on earth are portrayed from a heavenly perspective. The great persecution, even in its early stages, created fear among Christians, who lived with the constant danger of death. The souls of those who had already been martyred for "...the word of God and the testimony they had given" (6:9) were seen "under the altar." Christians who refuse to sacrifice at the altar of Caesar are priests who sacrifice themselves on the true altar of God, as Christ, the great high priest, sacrificed himself. The temple at Jerusalem was a shadow of this great heavenly temple, and here the martyrs dwell in the most sacred of places.

The carnage of persecution continues on earth. The martyrs already in heaven, not content with celebrating their own deliverance, cry out "How long?" (6:10) They cannot understand why God permits the suffering and killing to continue. Here is a cry for God to reveal himself, a plea for a public vindication of God's justice.[46] God is patient with evil-doers, but in the end there is no way to ignore the evil that is radically incompatible with God's nature.

The opening of the sixth seal reveals a picture of total calamity. The terrified inhabitants of earth call upon the mountains and the rocks to fall on them and hide them "...from the face of the one seated on the throne and from the wrath of the Lamb; for the great day of their wrath has come, and who is able to stand?" (6:16-17) They find out too late that there is such a thing as the wrath of God. Who can stand against the Almighty? God shakes his head and the universe trembles. Who can defy God and live? The description of carnage is a cry of anguish for justice and a vindication of the innocent martyrs.

---

[46] Psalm 79:5-10

The Redeemed Are Sealed

Chapter 7 answers the question of who can stand before the wrath of God. Whatever happens, Christ will protect His followers. One hundred forty-four thousand persons will be sealed with a stamp on their foreheads. The seal is a symbol of God's ownership; therefore, they are safe.[47]

One hundred forty-four thousand is 12 x 12 x 10 x 10 x 10. Twelve is the symbol of organized religion. One thousand represents human completion three times over. One hundred forty-four thousand is, then, a symbol of the complete, holy, universal church. All true members of the body of Christ will stand. Not one will be lost. John reports, "After this I looked, and there was a great multitude that no one could count, from every nation, from all tribes and peoples and languages, standing before the throne and before the Lamb…." (7:9) What a great heavenly scene following the ingathering from all parts of the earth!

Those who are sealed will not be spared hardship. Some will know grueling thirst and insufferable heat as they languish in prison cells. Others will experience the horrors of torture and the testing of fire. Many will die for the faith in the warfare between Christ and the opposing horsemen. All must battle on the side of the white horseman, assured that Christ on the white horse rides at their side and wears the crown of triumph.

---

[47] Ezekiel 9:4

God promised a great victory in heaven for the martyrs. There will be no tragic, haunting memory of suffering. Those who have come through the great tribulation and martyrdom shall wear robes of white bleached by the blood of Christ. They will go from the dark dungeon to the great white throne. There is a mighty, final victory in Christ, and in that day, "...God will wipe away every tear from their eyes." (7:17)

A Heavenly Benediction

As we leave this incredible scene it is fitting that we go with a wonderful prayer of benediction: "Amen! Blessing and glory and wisdom and thanksgiving and honor and power and might be to our God for ever and ever! Amen." (7:12)

Questions for Discussion

1. In what sense should the Church be at war? Have you considered the battle as being between Christ and the hunger or poverty of the poor?
2. Most hospitals in America were founded and owned by churches. Do you believe the impetus for healing the sick was the war against illness portrayed as Christ riding against the horseman on the pale horse? How do you react to the fact that 35 million Americans had not been able to afford health insurance before implementation of the Affordable Care Act?
3. Under what circumstances should Christians endorse and support war? Do you believe that God hates war? Can you explain the "just war"

doctrine developed by the Church across the centuries?

4. Do you see the suppression of the human spirit through force, threat, or disapproval as a form of spiritual violence? Under what circumstances?

Chapter 6

THE SILENCE OF HEAVEN

and

SIX TRUMPETS SOUNDED

Revelation 8, 9

Christians in the seven churches might have been tempted to think that God had not heard their prayers for deliverance. Did God care? They sent heavenward their plea: "O God, save the gospel in the earth; protect the weary, struggling churches; let your kingdom come on earth as it is in heaven."

The Hush of Expectancy (Revelation 8:1-7)

What was the response in heaven? The answer is found in the interim before the opening of the seventh seal. The music of heaven stops. The heavenly singers are suddenly quiet; a hush falls over heaven. We are near the anticipated end events. But instead of a final scene, there is a pause. After building a crescendo in his great Hallelujah Chorus, Handel wrote in a long pause, and then the final exploding "hallelujah." This is great music, and for John it was good theology. The end comes later. John remembers the words of the prophet Zephaniah, "Be silent before the Lord God! For the day of the Lord is at hand."[48]

Before the Lamb opens the seventh seal there is a silence of trembling suspense. It is the silence of expectancy. Will God answer the cry of His praying people? In the silence, all of the heavenly company can hear the prayers of God's people on earth. These prayers are more important to God than any activity in the celestial city.

All of the other prayers in Revelation are from heaven and are praise and thanksgiving to God and to the Lamb. As the universe waits breathlessly, an angel comes and stands at heaven's altar. The angel takes the prayers from earth and adds incense. The smoke of mingled incense and prayer rises before God.

These symbols say that God has heard the prayers of the saints on earth and is ready to respond. Notice how the scene portrays the absolute sovereignty of God, but at the same time the involvement of the people on earth. The profound truth behind this vision is that the Church on earth participates in working out God's will. The nature and timing of the end of history are determined, in part, by our prayers as they help to form God's plan.

---

[48] Zephaniah 1:7

Trumpets Are Warnings

With peals of thunder, flashes of lightning, and rumblings of earthquakes, God indicates that He will punish unjust rulers. But more importantly, God will first warn evil doers to turn from their sinful ways. The response from heaven is revealed through imaginative events announced by the blowing of seven trumpets. God answers the pleas of His people for a final demonstration of His Lordship.

The blowing of the trumpets in Revelation is analogous to the effect of the trumpet sound for a nation long under the heel of a vicious oppressor. After years of weary longing, one day the oppressed people hear trumpets. An army of liberation is approaching! The trumpets sound a warning of disaster to the oppressor, but they are the fanfare of freedom to the people under persecution.

Each time another angel blows a trumpet it begins a movement from heaven to earth, making clear that what happens is God's action. The vivid imagery alludes to scenes from the plagues imposed on Pharaoh in Egypt when he refused to free the Israelites, to historic disasters such as the volcanic eruption of Mount Vesuvius in 79 A.D. (8:8), to eclipses of the sun and moon, to red dust blowing in from the Sahara, as it did on occasion, and to real periodic plagues of locusts. The rhetoric here represents the terrible destruction needed to rid the earth of the influence of Satan. The language serves to shock the reader and perhaps turn those in power from their destructive course of action.

Some popular preachers today equate these signs with our abuse of creation, like making napalm bombs (8:7), atomic explosions (8:8), or acid rain caused by industrial pollution (8:10-11). John is not predicting our specific problems. However, the imagery can certainly and appropriately lead us to recognize the consequences of our destructive actions, and we can see these consequences as signs of God's judgment and a call for us to radically change our direction.

The First Four Trumpets (Revelation 8:7-13)

The trumpet series retells the story of God's anger and His positive response to the prayers of the Christians. There are both parallels and differences between the images in the opening of the seals and the images in the blowing of the trumpets. As examples, in the first series (opening of the seals) water becomes bitter; in the second series (blowing of the trumpets), water is turned into blood. In the "seals" series sun, moon and stars grow dark; in the "trumpet" series, the sun scorches the people. Both series are variations on an existing theme from Jewish tradition. John may have known two versions of this apocalypse; instead of choosing between them, he may have decided to present both. Some people today see this as a description of nuclear winter.

Each verse in the vision takes us back to an Old Testament scripture, or to one of the semi-canonical books known today as the Apocrypha. For example, the third trumpet turns part of the rivers and lakes to bitterness, as a great star falls from heaven. The reference is to Jeremiah's words, "...I am feeding this people with wormwood, and giving them poisonous water to drink."[49] Wormwood was an extremely bitter but not lethal herb with a medicinal ability to expel parasites, used as a symbol for the bitter suffering of God's people in the Hebrew Bible.[50]

"Then I looked, and I heard an eagle crying with a loud voice as it flew in midheaven, 'Woe, woe, woe to the inhabitants of the earth....'" (8:13) The image of an eagle, a far-sighted bird of prey, is yet another graphic way of portending disaster. There is also a reference to vultures circling overhead to feed on dead bodies.

Rather than destroying the earth completely, God is sending partial judgments. One third of the ocean, the rivers and the land are destroyed. The destruction of particular nations may be God's judgment on them. The sinful Roman Empire will decay and fall. The Christians need not fear. God's cause will not be destroyed.

The Fifth Trumpet (Revelation 9:1-12)

The fifth trumpet causes deadly plagues. These verses may be less confusing to us when we realize that John is using material from a long tradition. Indeed, he is combining material from three sources: (1) the tradition of the Egyptian plague of locusts;[51] (2) locusts

---

49 Jeremiah 9:15

50 Lamentations 3:15; Jeremiah 9:14

51 Exodus 10:12-20

becoming like men (as in Joel, where there is an attack on Zion by a demonic army of giant locusts that look like horses, riders and war chariots);[52] (3) the ancient tradition of the fall of an angel prince from heaven.[53]

To understand the imagery we must recapture the ancient belief that the world is flat and beneath the flat disk of earth is the underworld.[54] The underworld is joined to the earth's surface by a shaft, the entrance to which is sealed and guarded. This is the first glimpse in Revelation of the ancient picture of the underworld. The fallen angel, bent on destruction, is depicted as God's servant, doing His will. It is not that God wills evil. Rather, under God's law, the destructive consequences of evil actions will eventually cause so much destruction that the evil itself will be destroyed and through God's power turned to an ultimately positive end.

Smoke rises from this opened shaft (9:2-3), a reference from Joel.[55] We then learn (9:4) that locusts spring forth from the shaft. These locusts eat only human flesh, and only the flesh of those not in the community of faith. Next we are told that the plague kills only a part of the people and lasts for a limited time (9:5).

---

[52] Joel 1 and 2

[53] Isaiah 14:12; I Enoch 86:1

[54] 2 Peter 2:4

[55] Joel 2:10

Those who are tormented by the plague (9:6) will long for death.[56] These hybrid creatures, (9:7-10) are partly one animal and partly another. Some traits are borrowed from Joel (2:4); they have the appearance of war horses but they have the teeth of lions.[57] The sound of their wings is like the noise of many chariots.[58]

This demonic army of locusts has a ruler (9:11). His name is given in both Hebrew and Greek. Abaddon in Hebrew is the designation of the abyss, the place of the dead.[59] In Greek the word is "Apollyon" which means "the destroyer." This may be a reference to Apollo, one of the more complex Greek gods who, in addition to many positive attributes including god of the healing arts, was also considered the god of plagues and pestilence. He was the god of prophecy, speaking through the oracle of Delphi, who received his messages through fumes rising from a fissure in the earth. Domitian often likened himself to Apollo.

The Sixth Trumpet (Revelation 9:13-21)

The scene shifts, and this time a vast army comes not from the underworld but from east of the river Euphrates. First, there is a voice from heaven preparing the way for the action (9:13). The blowing of the trumpet releases four demonic angels that have been

---

[56] Job 3:21; Jeremiah 8:3

[57] Joel 1:6

[58] Joel 2:5

[59] Job 26:5, 6; Psalm 88:12; Proverbs 15:11

held in chains at the river Euphrates. In 1 Enoch 56, evil angels incite the nations of the East, Parthians and Medes, to invade Palestine with the purpose of destroying the people there. The Euphrates River was the eastern boundary of the Roman Empire. Even the great Roman Empire had grounds to fear ferocious barbarians just beyond its boundaries waiting for the right moment to invade. Once again, John takes a current anxiety based on actual contemporary circumstances and elevates it to an eschatological myth.

With his vivid imagination, John then pictures 200 million cavalry invaders swarming in from the East. They are demonic creatures with mythological characteristics. Horses and riders are one creature. The breastplates are in colors that correspond to fire (red), smoke (blue), and sulfur (yellow), like the sulfur and fire that destroyed the ancient cities of Sodom and Gomorrah.[60]

Beyond the sins of murder, adultery and theft is added the sin of sorcery (9:21). Sorcery played a large part in the popular religions of the Eastern Mediterranean; Jesus steadfastly refused to bow to the temptation of abusing his powers for any kind of self-aggrandizement or control over others. Through all the destruction is God's desire for humanity to repent (9:20-21). But despite the horror, rebellious humanity does not change.

---

[60] Genesis 19:24, 28

A Postscript

Barbarians invaded the city of Rome 410 years after the birth of Christ. Rome had not been invaded for a thousand years. Rome was called "the Eternal City." Gibbon, who wrote a monumental history of the Roman Empire, estimated that in its golden age the city had a million inhabitants. A few years after the invasion there were only forty to sixty thousand people remaining. Writers of that long-ago period told how they stood on the ruins of the old city and looked out over the countryside. For miles around they could see deserted estates of the Roman nobility, with bats and wolves inhabiting their marble villas.

One of the great thinkers of Christian history, St. Augustine, lived at the time when Rome was invaded. For ten years after the fall of Rome, while Augustine was writing his book *The City of God,* he considered the question of why Rome fell. Further, he asked, "What is the basis for any stable civilization?"

Augustine concluded that Rome's trouble was deep seated. The invasion of the Goths was not the real cause of Rome's fall. In former times the Goths would have been repelled. But for three hundred years the society had been in a state of decay. It was like a house that termites had been eating from the inside. It might appear sound on the surface, but during a windstorm or other challenge it would collapse. Rome fell because she was intent upon building the city of man and ignored the City of God. This disintegration is analogous to Paul's observation that "the wages of sin is death." (Romans 3:23b).

What Augustine analyzed in retrospect, the book of Revelation anticipated. The heavenly hosts waited in awe and suspense as they heard the prayers of Christians caught in persecution. There was silence in heaven for half an hour. How would God answer?

This I Believe

God said through these mythical visions that He does care; that He controls the future. God will try to save wayward humanity by bringing partial judgments to awaken humanity to repentance. If sinful people or nations refuse to respond, the natural decay caused by further injustice and debauchery will inevitably cause their defeat, and the Christian gospel will be freed from the oppression of satanic powers. Rome could not triumph over Christianity. Neither will any other evil force that comes forth on the earth. We rest assured that "the Lord God omnipotent rules forever and ever."

Does this judgment make Revelation a book of historical prophesy? Yes, in the sense that it shows how God works in history; no, in the sense that it is not a literal prediction of specific historical events.

Questions for Discussion

1. Is it possible to believe in the absolute rule of God and at the same time believe in free will for people? Are these seemingly opposite beliefs resolved for you here?

2. Do you understand the blowing of trumpets signaling great destruction as the acts of a vengeful God? Or, do you interpret this

devastation as the inevitable outworking of injustice and oppression, the hand of a just God?

3. How do you interpret movements such as the rise and fall of Communism? Did Communism gain power because of subjection and injustice toward the common people of Russia under the Czars? Did it fail because, in turn, it also oppressed the human spirit?
4. What forces help to explain the rise of Muslim extremism? What should be the strategy of the churches in helping overcome the anger and hatred expressed toward America?

Chapter 7

THE LAST TRUMPET SOUNDED

Revelation 10, 11

The newspaper reported that a wildcat strike in New York City tied up the subways during rush hour. Thousands of people hurried down the long stairways to the toll booths, only to be turned away. Everyone had to return to the street and seek other transportation. But the interesting part of the story was that most of those in the long line going up did not bother to tell those in the long line going down that they could not get on the trains. Many who were told wanted to check for themselves. Even people who knew about the strike pushed their way down the stairs.

This true story reveals a great deal about human nature. People make the same mistakes throughout history. Dozens of nations go down the same road to ruin. It might seem that we would learn from past mistakes, but most of us prefer to go on blindly, repeating the mistakes, and then paying the same price others have paid.

Summary and Preview

The two previous chapters dealt with the sounding of six trumpets. They heralded God's temporal judgment on nations and people who obstruct His will. Those trumpets were calls to repentance, localized judgments of God. People were invited to learn from their mistakes. But when the last trumpet sounds, those who have refused to learn and change must face a final judgment. Then the chance to repent has vanished. Before that fateful trumpet blast there are two dramatic interludes. As Chapter 7 was an interlude between the opening of the sixth and seventh seals, so Chapter 10 to Chapter 11:13 is an interlude between the sixth and the final trumpet. This interlude serves the double purpose of creating suspense and giving the church a powerful vision of its role during the time of persecution.

Revelation is fast action drama. It is a book of changing pictures. Every truth is presented through vivid imagery. In these two chapters the pictures change seven times in rapid succession. It is as if we had a series of seven short videos and played them one at a time on our screens. Let us, then, turn on our sets, watch the videos, and study their meaning.

The Dazzling Angel (Revelation 10:1-7)

The first scene is that of an angel coming down from heaven, bringing John a small scroll or book. The celestial messenger is clad in a cloud, dressed in brilliance. A modern impressionistic artist could copy the scene. The direct rays of the sun are diffused into all the colors of the rainbow, the symbol of hope. The legs of the angel are as columns of fire, such as led the children of Israel in the wilderness. The angel stands with one foot on the land and the other on the sea, symbolizing that the message is for the whole world. He cries with a loud voice, like the roar of a lion, so that all people will listen.[61] This vision reminds us once more that events are controlled from above, not from earth.

There is a loud rumble like seven peals of thunder.[62] Other instances in Revelation also depict thunder preceding God's acts of judgment.[63] Just as John begins to write what the thunder has to say he is told to seal the message (10:4). The reason is given: "...There will be no more delay, ...the mystery of God will be fulfilled...." Six trumpets have given ample warning. When the seventh trumpet sounds, God's final judgment will be pronounced. The angelic figure raises his hand to heaven and swears an oath by the eternal God to confirm that there will be no more delay. Once again, the imagery is taken from Daniel. There, an angelic figure raises both arms to heaven and states that the end time will be three and a half years. This angel also stands with one foot on the land and one on the water. But note the change in the prophecy. In Revelation the time frame is not three and a half years

---

[61] Amos 3:8. There are many other references to God speaking through thunder in the Old Testament.

[62] Psalm 29:3-9

[63] Revelation 4:5; 8:5; 11:19; 16:18

but "the time is at hand." Now the day of fulfillment is dawning.[64]

The Bittersweet-Tasting Book (Revelation 10:8-11)

The next video flashes onto the screen. John is taking the scroll from the hand of the angel and eating it. The angel has instructed him to swallow the scroll. He is told that it will be sweet to his taste but bitter to his stomach. (10:9) When the prophet Ezekiel began to prophesy, he swallowed a similar scroll. "It was in my mouth as sweet as honey."[65] He realized that it was a special honor to be a prophet of God, a very sweet taste, but the message he was given was about coming earthquakes, floods, and death. Ancient Israel was a hard hearted people. Ezekiel did not enjoy condemning his fellows; that was bitter medicine.

Today, as then, it is sweet to be a minister or priest entrusted with speaking the word from God. Every preacher knows that joy. Every preacher should know the sorrow of speaking truth to those who defy God. Any clergy person who speaks of God's judgment without a breaking heart is venting his/her own feelings of hostility rather than serving as a messenger of God. Nonetheless, it is the sacred calling of the clergy to prophesy, to speak God's judgment plainly, as well as to proclaim the hope found in God's love.

---

[64] Daniel 12:7-12

[65] Ezekiel 2:8 ff

The message about swallowing the book conveys John's role as prophet. John says he is not merely a spectator or a reporter; he becomes a vehicle of communication between God and His people. Nowhere else in the letter does John say he speaks as a prophet. His purpose is perhaps not only to confirm his own role, but also to establish the place of prophesy in the early New Testament community.

The Temple Measured (Revelation 11:1-2)

The third video still depicts the interlude between the sixth and seventh trumpets. It shows John measuring the temple in Jerusalem. He is told not to measure the outer courtyard, known to Jews as the Gentile court. That is to be given over to non-believers for forty-two months.

What is the meaning of this video clip?

Caesar controls the city for 1,260 days, half of seven years, or for an indefinite period of time, but the temple and those worshipping in it are spared. Not only are they spared; they continue to have the privilege of witnessing to the world around them. There is no implication that the earthly temple at Jerusalem was standing or would be rebuilt before a second coming of Christ. That temple had been ruthlessly destroyed, leveled to the ground by the Roman legions some twenty years prior to this letter.

The symbolic meaning is that the true worshippers of God, the Christians, will be protected during the persecution and during the subsequent judgments of God. God does not forget His people during times of tragedy. Those in the Gentile court do not belong to God's redeemed and do not have that spiritual protection.

The prophets of old foretold that the temple in Jerusalem would stand until the end of the ages. This prophecy was true, said John, but not in the way the people expected. It was the living temple of God's faithful people that would stand. Hence this temple could be measured even though the earthly center of Jewish worship had been destroyed.

The important point is that people must be inside the temple to be assured of safety. In the old Israel those who were on the fringes of Judaism were given recognition by being permitted a place in the outer court. But John says that now fringe faith is not enough. A person must be inside the temple. There is no neutral ground.

Two Powerful Witnesses (Revelation 11:3-6)

A quiet defensive protection against persecution is not enough. Christ in all his majesty must be positively proclaimed. Jesus had told his disciples not to put their candle under a bushel but rather to put it on a lampstand where the world might see it. The Church is not to hunker down during the persecution and wait for it to end. Christians are to preach and live the gospel at every level of their lives, as they continue to transform the world.

What is God's plan for extending the witness during the persecution? Two witnesses have power to prophesy for 1,260 days. This, again, is three and a half years, the time during which the outer courtyard is given over to the nations.

Now we are ready for the next video. There stand the two witnesses. They are human, yet they appear as olive trees. From another angle one might take them for two lampstands. This is a clear reference to a vision of the prophet Zechariah.[66] In that vision the olive trees represented to King Zerubbabel the word of the Lord, "Not by might, nor by power, but by my Spirit, says the Lord of hosts." The popular interpretation of Zechariah held that these two witnesses were Moses and Elijah, representing the law and the prophets. God protected and empowered them to witness in the midst of their enemies.

Dead Bodies and Gleeful Scorners (Revelation 11:7-14)

We learned in the first chapter of Revelation that lampstands represented the churches. The temple will be preserved, but the two witnesses are killed for their testimony. We flash the picture on the screen and see the dead bodies of the martyrs as they lie in the street. On one side is a great host of gleeful scorners who rejoice in their death, but at the top of the picture one discerns the eyes of the Eternal keeping watch over His own. "But after the three and a half days, the breath of life from God entered them, and they stood up on their feet, and those who saw them were terrified.... And they went up to heaven in a cloud while their enemies

---

[66] Zechariah 4

watched them." (11:11-12) Then followed an earthquake that destroyed part of the city and killed 7,000 people. The blood of the martyrs will fertilize the soil of God's wrath, and judgment will come upon those who mock.

The Last Trumpet (Revelation 11:15)

But wait. The picture is changing again. An angel steps forth with a trumpet to its lips. The angel blows a long, loud blast. The seventh and last trumpet has sounded! In heaven the four and twenty elders fall on their faces to worship God as a host of voices in the background shout in unison, "The kingdom of the world has become the kingdom of our Lord and of his Messiah, and he will reign forever and ever." (11:15)

This cry of victory is like a triumphant proclamation of the inevitable outcome. The remainder of Revelation describes the details of how the victory is won. It tells how the Emperor, Domitian, inspired by Satan, challenges the sovereignty of Christ, but the Savior responds to the challenge with a final victory. He then reigns forever.

The blowing of this trumpet is the great divide in the book of Revelation. In the Colorado Rockies there is a line called the continental divide. All rain or snow that falls on one side of this slope trickles down into little streams that become rivers and eventually empty into the Atlantic Ocean, while the water only a few feet away on the other side of the divide is destined to make its way to the Pacific Ocean.

Here is the great watershed, the decisive moment of Revelation, the climax of the drama. There remains the denouement, the manifestation of that which is inevitable. God has decided to act in response to the prayers of the people in the churches.

God's Covenant Made Final (Revelation 11:16-19)

The final video scene in this pictorial passage reveals God's temple in heaven. The "ark of the covenant" has been transported symbolically from the temple in Jerusalem, saying that God's covenant with His people is heavenly and eternal. The "ark of the covenant" was a gold-covered wooden chest built by Moses to house the tablets containing the Ten Commandments. It represented the agreement between God and His people to remain faithful to each other. Around the ark there are flashes of lightening, peals of thunder, earthquakes and heavy hail. God's wrath has flamed. God's judgment is sure. God's kingdom will come.

A Postscript

John Bunyan's book, *Pilgrim's Progress,* written in the 1660s, was the bestselling book in the English language for more than a century, except for the Bible. In Bunyan's allegory, the town of Vanity was along the road to the Celestial City. Christian and his companion, Faithful, found it necessary to pass that way on their pilgrimage. A fair was in progress in Vanity. Nations featured rows of booths where merchants sold corrupt wares. There were bribes, vice and folly that honest Christian and Faithful could not condone.

The pilgrims created a stir because they did not enter the booths of sin or so much as desire to look at the wares being offered for sale. The two were asked, "What will you buy?" The inquirers were abashed with the response, "We buy the truth."

The pilgrims were mocked because they wore Christian clothes and spoke the strange language of Zion. They were beaten, smeared with dirt, and cast into a cage. After a mock trial at which Mr. Blindman served as foreman of the jury, the two were condemned to death. Their godliness could not be tolerated.

Faithful took the shortest road to the Celestial City, as he was tortured and then martyred. (Bunyan was careful to add that "a chariot and a couple of horses waited to carry Faithful the nearest way to the heavenly gate.") Christian, on the other hand, was freed through the providence of God and was able to continue on his journey.

These two chapters of Revelation, through the symbols of measuring the temple and the two witnesses who were martyred, told the early church that some would be killed for their faith, especially the prophets, but all Christians were to continue in their appointed roles as part of the priesthood of all believers. Both the martyrs and those who remained were to be faithful witnesses, like the two travelers described by John Bunyan.

Questions for Discussion

1. Why would the prophet Ezekiel eat a book? Was it a common practice for Ezekiel to teach (prophesy) through acting out the message?

2. The basic role of the prophet was not to "foretell" but to "forth tell." The prophet was called to speak God's Word of Truth in actual situations, often speaking to political or religious leaders. Reflect on whether the minister or priest has a role as prophet.

3. Do you understand the temple or the church to be a building? Or is the church at a deeper level the community of people who worship there?

4. We can now conceive of the final destruction of planet Earth. Can we understand the blowing of the seventh trumpet as a signal that God's patience can run out with us? Is it time for humanity to heed warning signs of possible destruction? How? Can we understand this prophesy without seeing it linked to any specific historical event?

5. What should we do now as Christians to respond to God's message?

Chapter 8

WOMAN CLOTHED WITH THE SUN

and

THE SIGN OF THE SEALED

Revelation 12, 13, 14

In the era before Columbus sailed to the West many of the coins of Spain bore the words "Ne plus ultra" – "There is nothing beyond." Spain held the Pillars of Hercules on her shores. These huge boulders guarded the Mediterranean Sea from the vast unknown ocean beyond. Then Columbus came and with him the age of the explorers. America was discovered. The words on the coins had to be changed. "Ne" was removed, and later coins said only "Plus ultra" – "More beyond."

When the early church faced persecution from Caesar and his imperial priests who enforced emperor worship, they were tempted to think there was nothing beyond. But in that moment of doubt and fear John's vision revealed an eternal kingdom and an unseen ruler of this world. It was as if the Christians could now see and rejoice in "more beyond."

In these three chapters of Revelation Satan relentlessly pursues Christ, his mother, the Church, and indeed individual Christians, in a supreme effort to defeat them. Satan enlists the support of two beasts, representing (1) the Roman ruler and (2) his imperial cult to enforce emperor worship. Those who succumb to Caesar and emperor worship have the mark of the beast stamped on their foreheads, while those who faithfully follow Christ are sealed with the name of God and His Christ. The sealed are safe forever. The martyred are honored as heroes in heaven.

The Woman, the Dragon, and the Child (Revelation 12:1-18)

The first scene after "God's temple in heaven was opened" at the end of the previous chapter is the "great portent" of the woman clothed with the sun. She also has the moon under her feet and twelve stars for a crown. She is adorned with heavenly light. Representing Mary, the mother of Jesus, she is in the travail of childbirth.[67] The next portent to appear is a fierce dragon, the color of blood, representing Satan. He has seven heads and ten horns that symbolize his great power. He is determined to kill the unborn

---

[67] Traditionally Israel was portrayed as the wife of God. Now the Church becomes the bride of Christ. Many Old Testament passages refer to Israel as "a wife in travail: Isaiah 26:17; 66:7; Jeremiah 4:31; Hosea 13:13; Micah 4:10.

Christ-child, a son destined to rule the nations.[68] This ferocious dragon claws the earth before the apparently defenseless woman. The dragon sweeps a third of the stars from the sky in his attempt to kill the Christ-child.

The dragon crouches, ready to devour the infant as he is born. Satan recognizes that the birth of Jesus is the opening round in a battle that will be deadly and uncompromising. He will be weakened and ultimately defeated unless he can obliterate Jesus and later the churches. Can the mother and the child survive? Herod massacred the babies in an effort to kill Jesus. The woman is protected and nourished by God even though Satan seemed to have all the power on his side.

Just as the wily dragon is about to destroy the child, the infant is caught up into heaven. This is cosmic warfare in which heaven helps its own. The undaunted dragon carries the battle through the portals of Paradise. Michael and other protecting angels rush forward to expel Satan and his cohorts.

The Church of the Capuchins in Rome houses a famous painting by Guido Reni. It is an imaginative portrayal of this battle in heaven. Michael, the protector of heaven's gate, is dressed in shining armor. He stands victorious with his foot pressed hard on the dragon's head. In his hand is a flashing sword. Satan, the ancient serpent, writhes and struggles beneath the angel's foot. His face is distorted with rage as he lies there in ignominious defeat.

---

[68] Psalm 2

John uses a familiar myth here to make his point and teach his truth. The Greek Asia Minor variant of the story, popular in John's day, dealt with the goddess Leto. When Python, the great dragon, the oracle serpent of Delphi, learned that the unborn son of Leto, who was to be named Apollo, was destined to destroy him, he hid in waiting for the mother who was about to give birth. On the island of Delos, where the north wind blew Leto for safekeeping, she bore Apollo and his twin sister, Diana. After only four days, Apollo went forth seeking to slay the dragon. In this Greek version of the myth, the battle goes up to heaven and there the dragon is defeated.[69]

Again, the scriptural story is a symbolic picture, not an historical account. It is imagery, depicting Satan's consuming desire to destroy Christ. He will go to any length, even to heaven's gate, in his determination to conquer Christ. There, as elsewhere, he is soundly defeated.

We return to earth after the flight to heaven and discover that the mother has fled to the wilderness where she has other children who make up the church. Satan has lost his power in heaven (12:8-12). The child is safe. But Satan has decided to make Earth the final arena of a desperate battle.

His wrath is now focused on the woman. She is given the wings of an eagle to fly to the wilderness where she is to be nourished for a time (12:14). As

---

69 A reference to this myth is found in Isaiah 14:13-15.

Israel was miraculously fed with manna in the wilderness, so the infant church is nourished and kept alive by God.

Next Satan appears as a serpent who tries to drown the woman with a flood of water from his mouth, but Earth intervenes and absorbs the flood of water.[70]

Now the story takes a new twist. The dragon realizes that he cannot destroy the woman by a flood, so he turns to her other children. While the church itself cannot be destroyed, individual members may become martyrs.

To carry out this new scheme, the dragon stands on the edge of the sea (12:17). According to the common belief of people in that era, the sea symbolized chaos, evil and demonic powers; it was like the Roman Empire. The dragon decides to enlist the emperor to carry out his plan. Now ancient mythology is replaced with contemporary symbolism as John paints the picture of the desperate condition into which the Church has fallen.

Two Beasts from Sea and Land (Revelation 13:1-13)

Satan in the form of the dragon is depicted as giving his power to Caesar (13:1-10). This beast in its wielding of worldly power is described in similar terms as Daniel described a Hellenistic king who captured

---

[70] Psalm 32:6; 124:4-5

Jerusalem and forbade worship of Israel's God.[71] In Daniel's time, the Maccabees' revolt freed the Jews from that oppressive ruler. Many who fought the Romans in 70 A.D. had thought the Messiah would intervene to fulfill the vision of Daniel.

The vivid description of the first beast is taken directly from Daniel,[72] except that the characteristics of the four beasts in Daniel are combined into one beast in Revelation. You may recall the four kingdoms of Daniel were the Babylonians, the Medes, the Persians, and Diadochi, all rulers at the time of the Maccabees. The ten horns of the fourth beast in Daniel represented ten rulers, the last being Antiochus Epiphanes, the Diadochi ruler. In Revelation this first beast, combining the characteristics of the four beasts of Daniel, likewise refers to an historical situation. In Revelation, John uses the image of this beast to characterize the contemporary Roman Empire.

The first beast that rises out of the sea is the Emperor Domitian. He is cunning like a leopard, strong like a bear and dangerous like a lion. To this beast the dragon gives his throne. People worship the beast, saying, "Who is like the beast, and who can fight against it?" (13:4b)

Like the first beast, the second one (13:11) is also a servant of the dragon. The second beast has the task of getting earth's inhabitants to worship the first beast.

---

[71] Daniel 11:21-31

[72] Daniel 7:2-27

This is a clear reference to the Caesar priesthood that required all people to worship Caesar by putting incense on the altar and saying, "Caesar is Lord." There was a statue of Domitian in the temple at Ephesus. Scholars estimate that the statue was some 23 feet high. The head is still intact and is almost four feet tall. The statue was hollow, giving rise to the speculation that a priest of Caesar would hide inside and make the statue appear to talk. "…It deceives the inhabitants of the earth…." (13:14)

John next does something unusual at the end of his description of the second beast. He steps back from the vision to appeal directly to the reader. "This calls for wisdom: let anyone with understanding calculate the number of the beast, for it is the number of a person. Its number is six hundred sixty-six." (13:18)

The Mysterious Number 666

No other mystery in Revelation has given rise to more far-fetched speculation than the identity of this beast known by the number 666, called the Antichrist by some, though this term is not used in Revelation and appears only four times in the New Testament, all in 1 and 2 John.[73] How do we explain the mystery of this number?

There are two plausible explanations. In both the Hebrew and the Greek alphabets, each letter is given a numerical value. The number of a name could be ascertained by adding up the numerical values of the

---

[73] I John 2:18; 1 John 2:22; I John 4:3; 2 John 1:7

letters. In Pompeii, covered by volcanic ash for almost 1,900 years, scrawled on a wall were the words, "I love her whose number is 545."

It is not clear whether John is using Greek or Hebrew. He is probably a Palestinian Jew, as were most of his readers, having immigrated to Asia Minor. Using Hebrew, the sum of the letters in NERON QUESAR (Caesar Nero) adds up to 666. There was a popular belief among the Christians that the spirit of Nero was incarnated in Caesar Domitian.

But there is a second possible explanation, first given by Irenaeus in the second century. He turned simply to the symbolic nature of the number. As we have noted, seven is used constantly in Revelation and represents divine completion, while six is the sinister number, falling short of the sacred seven. Probably John had both symbols in mind, each reinforcing the other. Yes, Domitian was the spirit of Nero returned, and yes, Domitian headed a demonic, totalitarian state, falling miserably short of the divine plan that God is working out in history.

The Lamb and the 144,000 on Zion (Revelation 14:1-5)

Following the scene on earth, we return to the other side of the curtain. The Lamb stands on Mount Zion and with him are 144,000 persons who have the names of God and Christ sealed on their foreheads. Zion is a mythical place of protection and liberation. According to Isaiah, at the end of time God will be proclaimed king on Mount Zion. God's people will be liberated from oppression and death itself will be destroyed.[74] There follows another song from heaven. The 144,000 have been redeemed. They are the first fruits for God and the Lamb. This alludes to the custom in Israel of people giving the first fruits of their harvest to the priest at the temple as the tithe.

This passage ties directly to the earlier vision of the Sealing of the 144,000 (7:1-8). Members of the Church will be protected as God's own. They must remain faithful during the approaching trial. The 144,000 are not the perfected martyrs; but they symbolically represent the complete membership of the churches on earth. While they struggle against the emperor's oppression, they need to see their struggle from the divine perspective. The Lord is with them.

The Victory of the Sealed (Revelation 14:6-20)

The last passage in this section shows that God never forsakes the sealed. Angels appear to announce the destruction of the beast and the doom of those who receive his mark. The Son, sitting on the clouds, swings his sickle across the earth. His sharp judgment cuts down evil.[75]

Some scholars suggest that every participant in the Caesar cult had a "mark" tattooed on his or her hand and forehead. We do know for sure that worshippers of deities at that time frequently had themselves

---

[74] Isaiah 24:23; 25:8

[75] Daniel 7:11-14

tattooed or branded to identify themselves as the property of that deity. Slaves also bore the brand mark or tattoo of their owners. Roman Legions were marked as well. It may be helpful to note that the Greek word "charagma," translated "mark," denotes the official stamp of Caesar. There was a variety of "marking" practices in the culture.

At the time Revelation was written the Christians felt intense pressure to conform to the social norms of the larger culture. Most were Jewish Christians who had been forced to flee from Palestine twenty years earlier. Again, they brought with them a religion that proclaimed loyalty to a leader who had been crucified for being a threat to society. With the Emperor demanding supreme loyalty, the Christians were often forced to choose either to bow to Caesar or to stand with Christ.

John presents the stark choice made evident by two kinds of markings. Those who side with Caesar are marked with the number 666. In contrast, the faithful Christians who withstand Caesar's persecutions are sealed with the names of God and Christ written on their foreheads.

And there are profound consequences for choosing to worship Caesar rather than Christ. Anyone who worships the beast "…will also drink the wine of God's wrath, poured unmixed into the cup of his anger…." (14:9-11)

Postscript

During the American Civil War Juliet Ward Howe used the imagery of this fourteenth chapter of Revelation when she penned the words of "The Battle Hymn of the Republic." It helped to vindicate the Union army of the Civil War in its fight to strike down the evil of slavery.

> Mine eyes have seen the glory of the coming of the Lord.
>
> He is trampling out the vintage where the grapes of wrath are stored.
>
> He has loosed the fateful lightning of his terrible swift sword.
>
> His truth is marching on.

Questions for Discussion

1. What examples can you name of defenseless people pitted against great power, where the "David" overcame the "Goliath?"
2. Do you understand the warfare between Christ and Satan as literal or figurative? Is Satan a literal objective being, the fount of evil? Or does Satan metaphorically represent the evil impulses in every human heart?
3. Is there a single "Beast," or "Antichrist," at the end of history? Or have there been many powerful rulers who could be described as "Antichrist?" Do you share my view that the Beast of Revelation is Domitian, the Emperor?

4. Mormons and a number of fundamentalist Christian groups believe that a literal 144,000 persons will be "saved" with God's name stamped on their foreheads. How do you interpret the 144,000?
5. Do we live with cultural norms that are at odds with our Christian convictions? Does our church help us to deal with these issues?

Chapter 9

THE BATTLE OF ARMAGEDDON
Revelation 15, 16

The Setting

In the warm morning sunshine I rode along the highway from Mount Carmel to Nazareth. The flowers were blooming and the fields of grain waved in healthy splendor. Presently I found myself on the Plain of Esdraelon. The mountains of Moab rose in the distance, while to the right and closer at hand were the mountains of Gilead.

My Israeli companion explained that this rich plain is now "the breadbasket of Israel." I remembered how the fertile soil in this valley had been a prize for invading armies across the centuries. My friend remarked that we were riding through the oldest battlefield in recorded history. "Also," he added, "it was a battlefield in the recent war until Israel drove the Palestinians from the land."

Then I saw a highway marker pointing down a side road. The sign read, "Armageddon 3 miles." I was overwhelmed by the panorama of history that swept across my mind. This was one of the oldest and newest battlefields of history, but also the place that symbolizes the last great battle of history between Christ and Satan.

At Armageddon a decisive battle of Israel's early history ended in victory. Centuries later, however, two of Israel's most popular kings met death there because of disobedience to God.

I recalled how Barak had won a resounding victory over the Canaanites. The battle was immortalized in the song of Deborah. [76] I also remembered how Josiah went into battle against Neco, King of Egypt, in the plain of Megiddo. God spoke through the conscience of Josiah and told him not to fight this battle, but in his rebellion he disguised himself as an ordinary soldier and went forth to fight. An Egyptian sharpshooter arched his bow. The arrow sped to its mark and Josiah lay mortally wounded. His thirty-one year reign as a popular king was ended.[77]

To the descendants of Abraham, and to their spiritual heirs in the New Testament churches of Asia Minor, Armageddon was more than a hill on a plain. It symbolized the mount of God's rule. Thus the writer of Revelation was inspired to make Armageddon a symbol of Christ's final and complete victory. This modest crossroad in modern Israel is the lasting sign of God's power over history.

---

[76] Judges 4:14-16, Judges 5. The chariots were gathered "unto the river of Kishon," near the Plain of Megiddo.

[77] 2 Chronicles 35:22-24 and Zechariah 12:11 refer to this battle that had become a poetic symbol of deepest grief.

Preview

The vision of the seven trumpets is complete. The final call to repent ended with the blowing of the last trumpet. Chapter 15 is an interlude in which we again turn our attention from a description of doom to focus on the victory of the martyrs in heaven. Then in Chapter 16 we learn about the seven bowls of God's wrath poured out on all who oppose Him. Finally, there is that last great battle between Christ and Satan at Armageddon. These two chapters should be studied as a unit. Again, the purpose is to strengthen the resolve of Christians in the churches to remain faithful.

The Victory of the Martyrs (Revelation 15:1-8)

We are in heaven once again. After being introduced to a third set of plagues (15:1) John is privileged to see a multitude of martyrs. The hymn they sing is "the song of Moses...and the song of the Lamb." At the time of Israel's deliverance on the far side of the Red Sea, Moses sang a hymn of praise for deliverance. [78] The one sung in heaven (15:3-4) differs markedly from the original. We recall that John was writing from memory without the aid of a scroll. But the point is clear. Just as Israel was delivered from the Egyptians by Moses, so now Christ delivers the salvation community from the power of Caesar. The hymn of praise to Christ is taken mostly from Psalms[79]

---

[78] Exodus 15:1-18

[79] Psalm 98 and Psalm 111, for example

and describes the magnitude of God's works and His faithfulness. "Great and amazing are your deeds, Lord God the Almighty! Just and true are your ways, King of the nations! Lord, who will not fear and glorify your name? For you alone are holy. All nations will come and worship before you, for your judgments have been revealed." (15:3-4)

This time when the portals of heaven open we see "the tent of witness," the place where God dwells. In the long trek through 40 years of wandering in the wilderness, the Israelites carried a tent that housed the "ark of the covenant" and a chair called the "mercy seat" on which they believed God sat.[80] Symbolically, this sacred tent is now in heaven.

The seven angels process from the sanctuary with the seven bowls of wrath. All of heaven participates in worship and expectancy (15:7) as God places the full weight of His holiness behind this event. (15:8)

The Pouring Out of Seven Bowls of Wrath (Revelation 16:1-12)

In Chapter 16 we read that seven bowls of wrath were poured out, signifying the destruction of Babylon. In the punishment brought by the seven trumpets we recall that one third of the earth, the sea and sky was destroyed. These were localized punishments for sin and were meant to be calls to repentance. Now the final wrath of God is poured out on the whole corrupt

---

[80] Exodus 25:10-22; Hebrews 8:5

Roman Empire. Again, seven dreaded disasters were based on the plagues sent upon Egypt when Pharaoh refused to free the children of Israel. We see a coming exodus from the oppression of Babylon/Rome.

Many Old Testament images refer to God's wrath being poured out.[81] The first bowl was poured out upon the entire earth and caused a fearsome plague of sores on all who were marked with the sign of the beast. The second angel emptied his bowl into the sea; it became like the blood of dead men and all marine life died. The third bowl polluted rivers and other fresh water, making them as blood, leaving no drinking water (16:4). The fourth angel poured his bowl on the sun; people were scorched with fire (16:8-9). The fifth plague fell on the throne of the beast, casting his kingdom into darkness and chaos. The sixth angel, once again, centered his bowl of wrath on the river Euphrates, drying up the water and opening a passage for armies of the east to invade the Roman Empire. (16:12) In the year 530 B.C., the Persian king Cyrus diverted the course of the Euphrates river and marched his troops over a dry river bed to capture Babylon. We can interpret this passage as a statement that people receive their due. Justice is not inflicted by an arbitrary, vengeful God. Rather, we understand that our actions have consequences. The Greek text does not speak of punishment, but of judgment and justice.

---

[81] Psalm 69:24; Jeremiah 10:25; 42:18; 44:6; Zephaniah 3:8

The Mount of God's Victory

Between the pouring out of the sixth and seventh bowl of wrath we are introduced to three "foul spirits like frogs."[82] They come from the mouths of the dragon and the two beasts. Satan, Domitian, and the Council to Enforce Emperor Worship have spit out the frogs of political pressure, propaganda and deceit to discredit the Christians. Those evil ones conspire to unite their forces against Christ and the churches (16:13-14).

This is indeed the midnight hour. Then suddenly John hears someone speaking. The voice is that of the captain of salvation. "See, I am coming like a thief!..." (16:15) The scene shifts and we find ourselves at Armageddon, the mount of God's victory. The forces of Christ and Satan encamp on the plain near the mountain and gird themselves for a final struggle.

The Meaning of Armageddon

Those who interpret Revelation as a blueprint for the future say that Armageddon is the last literal battlefield of history. The flesh and blood forces of a present historical evil world ruler will battle the Christians who are living at that time.

Others, who see the book as a literal outline of history with each chapter representing a period of time, believe the three frogs are three influential false teachers. They have been described in modern times as the Pope, the World Council of Churches, and the Greek

---

[82] Exodus 8:2

Orthodox Church. Others say they are political leaders such as Hitler, Stalin, and then Saddam Hussein. Such interpretations would have had no meaning to those in the churches to whom the book was written, and are better rejected as modern fantasies.

The Armageddon of Revelation is not a place on a map ten miles from Nazareth. It is a symbol for a worldwide battle between Christ and Satan. It points to the ultimate struggle between good and evil. We do not expect to turn on the evening news and see an army headed by a beast with seven heads and ten horns. Neither do we expect to hear the news that three frogs are clearing the path to the battle. Through the ages there are wars, famines, pestilences, evil rulers and corrupt churches. All of them are opponents of Christ in the continuing spiritual warfare, which goes on until the end of time. Finally, the climactic showdown reveals Christ as victor over Satan. Truth conquers falsehood. Light overcomes darkness. Love is stronger than hatred. The key verse is 16:17. "...It is done." This is the same cry uttered by Jesus on the cross. Caesar is defeated! God rules!

This I Believe

It would be inconsistent with the life and teachings of Jesus to consider Armageddon as the place of an actual battle. Jesus refused to take the sword. He went meekly to the cross. He used a shield of faith and fought with a weapon that Paul called "the sword of the spirit."[83] There is no indication in scripture that Jesus will come with a conquering legion to slaughter those who have been his enemies. The battles of Christ are fought on the spiritual plains of the heart rather than with physical weapons on literal battlefields. Death and destruction caused by wickedness are always present, but this is the inherent fruit of evil, not the arbitrary sword of the Lord. We are reminded once more that Christians practiced complete pacifism during the first three centuries and that the hearts of multitudes of people in the empire were won in large part by demonstrations of love that replaced violence. The battle of Armageddon is a spiritual battle.

Postscripts

Tertullian of Carthage converted to Christianity in 196 A.D. He expressed in immortal words the method of Christian warfare during the persecution that he witnessed: "We have a battle, in that we are summoned to the tribunals, that we may then at the hazard of our life contend for the truth.... When we are slain, we conquer, and when we are crushed we escape. You may now call us faggot-men and half-axle-men because being bound to the wood of half an axle we are burnt by a circle of faggots enclosing us. This is the goal of our conquest; this is our robe of victory; in such a chariot do we triumph."

The truth of Armageddon is illustrated in the experience of Julian the Apostate, Roman emperor from

---

[83] Ephesians 6:10-20

361 to 363 A.D. Julian was the last pagan ruler who opposed Christianity. When he became emperor, he ordered all churches closed and he banned Christians from public office.

Julian led a Roman army to war in Persia. He stopped en route for six months near Antioch to gather supplies and train his troops. The emperor visited the city one day, disguised as a philosopher. He noted that his order to close all Christian churches had been obeyed. Rubble was heaped in front of the door of the church building where he stood. An observer detected a flicker of satisfaction across his face as he noticed that the pagan temples of Mithras were overflowing with worshippers.

As Julian strolled further down the street in Antioch, he bumped into an old childhood friend, now a leading merchant of the city. The man was a Christian and Julian had heard of his conversion. After a greeting, the Emperor taunted him, "Tell me, where is the Carpenter of Nazareth these days? I don't see him around. Are there not some small buildings he is being asked to build?"

The Christian merchant is said to have looked the pagan emperor squarely in the eye and replied, "The Carpenter of Nazareth is busy building a coffin in which to bury your empire."

Julian laughed, but not for long. He was killed on a slaughter field in Persia, and the next emperor ruled as a Christian. Julian was on the wrong side of history.

The Battle in Our Imagination

In imagination we climb the mountain overlooking the plain of Megiddo. From this vantage point we can see the battlefield below. From where we stand, we discern that the forces of God are stronger than the opposition, although this is not apparent to those who are on the field making ready for battle.

The life and death struggle begins. The canons fire. The tanks rumble forward. Airplanes swoop overhead. Bombs whistle to the earth and explode with a thunderous roar. The united forces of evil fight with might to subdue the forces of Christ. Not until the day of history fades into twilight is the last gun fired. Then, as a gentle breeze lifts the smoke away, we shout for joy. There stands Christ with his hosts in valiant victory!

Questions for Discussion

1. Do you understand the battle of Armageddon as symbolic, fought on the spiritual plains of the heart? If so, is it still for you a real battle and a most serious one?

2. The outcome of the battle signifies that Christ is stronger than Satan. Put another way, good is stronger than evil. God's will and plan for humanity is stronger than any opposition. Do you find strength and assurance in this concept? Do you believe it is true?

3. These chapters take us to heaven again, with the scene of a tent housing the "ark of the covenant" and the ancient mercy seat. How important

were the tent, the ark (box) and the seat that were carried by the Israelites? What did they symbolize?

4. What stories have you heard about the Battle of Armageddon?
5. Is it your deepest assurance that ultimately God's love conquers all?

Chapter 10

THE WOMAN IN SCARLET
Revelation 17, 18

In the first century crisis the Christians found it impossible to worship the emperor, Domitian. He was a mortal man and only God deserved worship. Therefore, Christians were urged to oppose that government. But the issues related to Roman rule were broader than emperor worship. In these chapters, John looks beyond Domitian to the unjust structure and corrupt style of government throughout the empire.

Rome as the Woman in Scarlet (Revelation 17:1-7)

The fall of Rome is the theme of these chapters. The first section again identifies Rome as Babylon and announces her fall. The next chapter is a lament for the destroyed city. As happens throughout Revelation, John draws sharp contrasts between the state and the church. In its outward appearance, Rome is glamorous and mighty, while the church is plain and weak. But in reality Rome is a harlot dressed in scarlet presiding over a city in the process of destruction. This woman, representing earthly power and corrupt materialistic values, contrasts by implication with the church, later described as the chaste bride of Christ, the Holy City, the New Jerusalem. Rome is dressed in fashionable purple, symbol of wealth and royalty, while the church is clothed in simple pure white linen.

An angel carries John to the wilderness. He goes there not because Rome is located in a desolate place but because the wilderness is traditionally a place where one goes to find clarity of thought. From that vantage point the early Christians see the city in true perspective. Describing a city as a woman was commonplace in Jewish history. Jerusalem was portrayed as a virgin,[84] a faithful wife and mother,[85] and as a married woman who became unfaithful.[86] Nineveh and Tyre were described as harlots.[87]

Many Romans considered the goddess Roma to be the giver of all blessings, just as Greeks worshipped Athena. Archeologists have uncovered temples to the goddess Roma in Ephesus, Smyrna and Pergamum.[88] But in Revelation the goddess is not a blessed mother; rather she is the woman in scarlet.

The harlot sits upon the waters and entices the kings of the earth to join her in emperor worship. The waters symbolize the people over whom she reigns.

---

[84] Isaiah 37:22; Lamentations 2:13

[85] Isaiah 66:7-14

[86] Ezekiel 16

[87] Nahum 3:1-7 and Isaiah 23:15-17 respectively

[88] Boring, M. Eugene, ***op. cit.***, p. 179

This infamous woman rides on a scarlet beast with seven heads and ten horns. The beast is the Roman Empire. An angel explains that the heads of the beast are seven mountains; Rome, of course, was built on seven hills. The ten horns represent the lesser kings throughout the empire who serve as vassals to Rome. The scarlet woman is dressed in splendor; Rome was a magnificent city as well as a wicked one. On her forehead is written, "Babylon the great, mother of harlots and of earth's abominations." (17:5) The woman is drunk with the blood of the saints (17:6).

The woman in scarlet was an incarnation of ancient Babylon, a place of worldly wealth and power where the Israelites had been held captive for more than 70 years. Even as that ancient city was destroyed and the children of Israel released from captivity, so the city of Rome will be destroyed and Christians will be freed from their tribulation.

The Self-Destructive Nature of Evil (Revelation 17:8-18)

John invites the reader to imagine two bizarre pictures of evil that help us discern the power behind Rome and indicate that the city is already doomed. (17:8-11) These pictures are not meant to predict future historical events but rather to reveal the nature of God's final victory. In the first picture, (17:12-14) the beast is defeated in a direct confrontation with the Lamb, as are the ten kings. Evil is automatically doomed to defeat. In the second picture (17:15-18) evil is defeated in a self-destructive battle. John's imagination now takes a new turn. The beast and its allies turn against Rome; the ten kings rebel and destroy the city. The message is that unjust rulers will create enemies and eventually fall. Those who live by the sword will die by the sword.

The Fall of Babylon (18:1-24)

By now you are not surprised to learn that this dirge over the fall of Babylon is composed by John using material from various Hebrew Bible laments. Cities that opposed Israel were perceived as enemies of God's people and were destroyed.[89] John is saying that the eschatological destruction of evil has long been predicted by prophets from Israel's past.

Rather than study Chapter 18 one verse at a time, I use a helpful summary from M. Eugene Boring.[90] There are four reasons presented in this section as the rationale for God's judgment on Rome. First, Rome is condemned for the way she makes her wealth and the way she uses it. Christians are under economic pressure to participate in trade guilds that are fraught with ungodly practices and the worship of local gods. Injustice in the courts is such that Christians automatically lose their cases when their identity is discovered. But Babylon is condemned here on wider issues. She lives in luxury at the expense of the poor. Merchants profit from aligning themselves unfairly with Rome. "The merchants have grown rich with the wealth of her wantonness." (18:3) Political and

---

[89] Isaiah 13;19; 23:1-16; 34:8-14; 47:9-11; Zechariah 2:9-12

[90] Boring, M. Eugene, ***op. cit.***, p. 186-188

economic ties between Rome and a merchant class in the provinces fostered the growth of wealth for a select few. Historians point out that never before had a people achieved the level of prosperity of the Roman Empire of the first century. But only certain social classes were reaping this wealth. A heavy burden of taxes impoverished the majority of people in Asia Minor. Most of the urban population lived in poverty (18:13). The author of Revelation sides with the oppressed majority.

Second, Rome is condemned for her blasphemous self-glorification. She "...glorified herself..." (18:7) rather than God. She sees herself as an eternal city. "I rule as a queen;...and I will never see grief." Her wantonness and gaudy luxury are forms of arrogance.

Third, the emperor cult promoted idol worship—an issue we have dealt with throughout this book. This is what John meant when he called Rome "Babylon" and described her as a harlot, charging her with fornication. This is quite simply a breach of the first commandment.

Finally, Rome used violence as her mode of operation, including the death penalty for Jews and Christians in matters of conscience. Those who resisted emperor worship were subject to death. But Roman violence went beyond "the blood of prophets and saints." It included "all who have been slain on earth." (18:24) Rule by violence is condemned; Babylon became a synonym for such rule.

But much about Rome is good. There is pathos in the lament that the joyous sound of music and the glad voices of the bride and groom are to vanish and be replaced by a dead and haunted city (18:21-23). The poet walks among the ruins and sings God's victory hymn with a heavy heart.

Vassal rulers received favors and advancements by going along with the corrupt Roman system. Likewise, merchants built their financial profits by making deals with government officials. God pronounced His wrath against unscrupulous persons who make big profits from corrupt business deals.

The second angel told God's people to separate themselves from the polluted life of the empire. "Come out of her, my people, lest you take part in her sins." (18:4) The "woman in scarlet" was so corrupt that Christians should have as little as possible to do with the state.

Conditions in the empire had changed little by the year 200 A.D. when Tertullian wrote, "I owe no duty to forum, battlefield, or Senate house; I stay awake for no official employment; I take notice of no councils; I avoid the voting booth; I wear out no magistrates bench.... I perform no military service; I govern nobody; I have seceded from the populace."

On the other hand, the pastoral letters of 1 and 2 Timothy and Titus admonish Christians to pray for those in authority. "...I urge that supplications, prayers, intercessions, and thanksgivings be made for everyone, for kings and all who are in high positions, so that we may lead a quiet and peaceable life in all godliness and dignity."[91]

This I Believe

Under the circumstances of Roman culture and imperial rule, it was appropriate for Tertullian and other Christians in Asia Minor to "come out of her," to refuse to participate in political life. But it would be a grave mistake to make this a mandate for all times or suppose that Christians today in our country should not participate in community and government affairs. Indeed, quite the opposite; we have a responsibility to stand up for our convictions and concerns by taking our place in the political and community arenas.

Christians, then, need a guiding principle when deciding whether to participate in government—or any organization. We join those groups for which we feel responsible and that in general support our Christian perspective. In any organization, we may object to some particular policies or practices. We do not need to resign so long as we can make our voices heard and share our views with others, while acknowledging our need to learn from others. We should separate ourselves, however, when we can no longer bear effective witness. If the group has become overwhelmingly corrupt, or if we can no longer support the basic direction of the group, we can witness more effectively by withdrawing than by working for internal

---

[91] 1 Timothy 2:1-2

reform. The basic principle is clear: separate from sin while making a loving witness.

Some modern scholars criticize John for drawing such a sharp line between church and culture. The Christians were urged to practice a purity of life that inevitably brought them into conflict with both state and culture. The church paid a terrible price for its obstinacy. It is estimated that in the first 400 years after Christ, as many as 1,950,000 Christians may have been martyred.

But the case can be made that it was precisely this steadfast adherence to the gospel that led to the incredible spread of the faith. By the year 400 A.D., twelve generations after Christ, a few generations after the Emperor Constantine had made Christianity the state religion, the world was almost 20% Christian, and the scriptures had been translated into eleven languages.[92]

The Council of Nicea

Constantine was the first Roman Emperor to convert to Christianity, after he had a vision of seeing a cross in the sky before an important battle in 312 A.D. Today a lonely hillside near Trier in western Germany has a cross and a monument claiming this to be the place where Constantine was converted.

In October 325 A.D. Constantine convened the great Council of Nicea. Three hundred Christian

---

92 Kenneth Curtis, *Church History Institute*, Issue 65, Wooster, Pa.

bishops from all parts of the empire assembled to work toward a creed that would express the essential doctrines and, hopefully, the unity of the Church. Modern Protestants, Roman Catholics, and Greek Orthodox still consider this creed to be the orthodox expression of their faith.

As Constantine entered the great oblong hall where the Council of Nicea met, he saw the assembly of 300 bishops, many of whom had endured persecution under Diocletian before Constantine became Emperor. The bodies of many had been mutilated by torture. The right eyes of many had been gouged out. Others were crippled from having had their legs in chains. Constantine saw these reminders of faithful witness, bishops who had endured persecution but brought the churches to a role of primary influence in the Roman Empire. The Church had, in fact, turned the world upside down.

Postscript

Mary Queen of Scots determined to rule Scotland as a Roman Catholic domain. At the same time, John Knox was trying desperately to free Scotland from what he considered to be the oppressive tyranny of Catholicism. As the minister of Saint Giles Cathedral in Edinburgh, he prayed, planned and preached for a protestant reformation. After hearing the complaints that John Knox was beginning to rule Scotland from the pulpit of Saint Giles, the Queen summoned the preacher to a confrontation at nearby Holyrood Palace. Mary opened the conversation by saying she felt Knox was sinning by teaching the people a religion different from her own. She asked him, "How can your doctrine be of God, seeing that God commands subjects to obey their rulers?"

Knox answered, "Madam, as right religion took not authority from worldly princes, but from God alone, so are not subjects bound to frame their religion according to the appetites of their princes." Knox then gave examples from scripture and church history to show that people must obey God rather than rulers. Mary inquired, "Think you then that subjects, having the power, may resist their princes?"

Knox replied boldly, "If the princes exceed their bounds, Madam, it is no doubt that they may be resisted, even by power. No greater honor is to be given kings than God has commanded to be given father and mother. But the father may be stricken with a frenzy in which he would slay his children. Now, Madam, if the children arise, apprehend the father, take away the sword, bind his hands and keep him in prison till the frenzy is over, think you that the children do wrong? Even so, it is with princes that would murder the children of God that are subject to them."

Mary, after a long period of silent amazement, answered, "Well then, I perceive that my subjects shall obey you, and not me."

Knox is said to have then stated fervently, "God forbid that ever I take upon me to command any to obey me; but my travail is that both princes and subjects obey God."

This conversation between a strong-minded queen and a stout-hearted preacher illustrates the dilemma when the government makes demands that are perceived to be against the will of God. The Christians in the churches in Revelation had clear guidance on how to respond.

Questions for Discussion

1. Do you respect persons who place their religious beliefs above obeying the laws of their country? Under what circumstances?
2. In what sense do you believe that evil is self-destructive? Is God's judgment on nations or systems of belief based solely on the degree to which they thwart "liberty and justice for all?" What is the basis for God's judgment? What was it for Rome in these chapters?
3. Do you understand God's judgment and wrath against economic structures that make some people extremely rich while keeping others poor? Can established economic practices be inherently opposed to the nature of God?
4. Can America sin by self-glorification? How?

Chapter 11

THE RETURN OF CHRIST
Revelation 19, 20

The book of Revelation provides us with many symbols of victory. "The Second Coming of Christ" is a watchword that points us beyond mere fate to faith in the living God. It assures struggling peoples that Christ has heard their cries. The Second Coming of Christ is our assurance that at the end of the journey there awaits One whom we revere and love. These chapters claim that Christ will stand at the end of history and usher humanity into his eternal kingdom, whether on earth or in heaven.

The Hallelujah Chorus (19:1-8)

We witness another breathtaking multi-layered drama, as though in an enormous movie theater with huge screens and glorious sound. This last section of the Book of Revelation deals with the consummation of history. The great multitudes in heaven once again join their voices in song, this time in a mighty hallelujah chorus: "...Hallelujah! Salvation and glory and power to our God." (19:1) "Hallelujah" is the language of praise and worship. At this point the boundaries between heaven and earth grow thin. A voice from the throne invites all of God's servants, including the hearers/readers in the churches, to join the chorus. "And from the throne came a voice saying, 'Praise our God, all you his servants, and all who fear him, small and great.'" (19:5) What is happening? It is not Caesar who controls the lives of the readers, "...For the Lord our God the Almighty reigns." (19:6)

Wedding Preparations (Revelation 19:8-9)

Next we learn that heaven is joyfully preparing for a wedding, "...for the marriage of the Lamb has come, and his Bride has made herself ready." (19:7) The Bride will be dressed in a fine white linen robe. This announcement points to a joyous coming event, but it also serves again as an invitation. The present time is still for courtship, promise and engagement. Here the "Bride" is the universal Church, whereas in Paul's letters the bride was the existing church on earth.[93]

Status of Angels (Revelation 19:10)

John bows to worship the angel who communicated the revelation (19:10). But the angel rebukes John, saying that he, like John, is simply a servant of God. We know that in some of the churches angels were exalted and dangerously confused with Christ.[94] John apparently added this aside to keep the churches from developing too high a view of angels.

---

93 Romans 7:2-4; 2 Corinthians 11:2 ff.; Ephesians 5:25 ff.

94 Colossians 2:18; 2 Corinthians 11:14

The Second Coming, Parousia (Revelation 19:11 to 22:5)

From Revelation 19:11 to 22:5 there are seven distinct and different visions of the end. They are: (1) the return of Christ, (2) the last battle, (3) the binding of Satan, (4) the thousand year reign, (5) the defeat of Gog and Magog, (6) the last judgment, and (7) the coming of the New Jerusalem. Here, as throughout the book, the visions appear in groups of seven. The order of the scenes is only loosely chronological. They merge, overlap, and are strikingly visual. John develops his vision of the culmination of history, again, in a flow of impressionistic video-like images. Each scene says something important about the end; none is to be taken literally.

Christ Comes On a White Horse (Revelation 19:11-21)

The first scene depicts what is often called the "second coming of Christ," though this is not a Biblical term. Heaven's gates open and a warrior on a white horse rides forth, leading armies from heaven. He is the Messiah who is coming to rule the nations with a rod of iron.[95] He wears a robe dipped in the blood of life.[96] Note that those who ride with him are not dressed for battle but for the victory celebration. They are clothed in pure white linen. On his head are many diadems; he

---

[95] Psalm 2:9

[96] Isaiah 63:1-6

is the rightful sovereign, "King of kings and Lord of lords." (19:16b) Jesus needs no warriors in this battle. He carries no instruments for fighting except the sharp two-edged sword in his mouth, the word of truth. The battle is decided before it begins.

John does not bother to depict the battle itself. The beast and the kings of the earth with their armies are captured. Along with a false prophet, they are cast into the lake of fire, while their soldiers are killed and the birds gorge on their flesh (19:21). After great battles vultures always flock to the fields to feed on the bodies of dead warriors.

Satan Is Shackled – For A While (Revelation 20:1-3)

The scene shifts in Chapter 20. An angel comes down from heaven with a rope and a key. Without a struggle the angel binds Satan, whose time has come, and casts him into the abyss. Three verbs are telling: "threw," "locked," and "sealed." (20:3) These descriptive verbs have the ring of our "signed, sealed and delivered."

The scene of Satan being bound for a thousand years has its source in Persian mythology, in a tale that portrays an evil serpent, Asi-Dahaka, being chained at the End. Isaiah perhaps echoed this myth in prophesying that the power of evil would be contained.[97] The evil kings, he said, "will be gathered

---

[97] Isaiah 24:21-23

together like prisoners in a pit; they will be shut up in a prison, and after many days they will be punished." As in Revelation, this is a temporary prison before the final trial and sentence. However, in Revelation, Satan will be released after 1,000 years and be allowed to deceive people again for a while.

The Millennium (Revelation 20:4-6)

The only place in the Bible where we hear of a millennium is in Revelation 20:4-6. Ten is the symbolic number for human completion; the millennium (10 x 10 x 10 years) is the time needed to complete the work of Christ in history. John gives us a vivid impression of a Satan-free world in which Christ is present with his people. No more will the nations be deceived. God's people are not inherently evil; they have been victimized by evil social structures and wicked rulers with whom their lives have been enmeshed. While there is a susceptibility to evil in the human heart, there is also an inherent goodness. Humanity was created in the image of God. There is no ultimate dualism. The power of evil is temporary, not eternal.

After Satan is bound, martyred Christians are raised from the dead and reign with Christ on earth as priests and kings for the thousand years. Others await a resurrection a thousand years later, in this scenario.

This I Believe

Although the concept of the millennium has attracted a great deal of attention from some, it is a very small scene in John's long vision. It occurs only in this one brief passage of two verses. It is an abuse of scripture to make the millennium a centerpiece of the book of Revelation, or indeed, of Christian theology. Like the picture of the "Second Coming," which also receives little space, the millennium is only one of John's many ways of portraying the End, or the culmination of history.

Later interpreters who misunderstood John's pictorial imagery and impressionistic style of representing great truths tried to make these pictures into objective history. They developed terms like "premillennial" (Christ returns to earth before the millennium after a time of cataclysmic destruction), "postmillennial" (Christ returns to earth after a thousand years during which the world has evolved into the kingdom of God), and "a-millennial" (the scripture does not portray a literal millennium before or after a literal return of Christ).

I am not forced to choose among these options because, as is clear by now, my own conviction is that the whole debate is based on misunderstanding. Again, this is not an historical account. It is a theological message portrayed in vivid imagery.

To make this into an objective historical event is like making the Garden of Eden story into history. Instead of focusing on the theological meaning of the story, the literalists get tied up defending the universe as being only six thousand years old.

Millennialism in Hebrew History

No one picture of the End does justice to John's message. The whole array of images must be permitted to be impressed on our imagination. To help us "get the picture" we must remember that the idea of a millennial period was part of an ancient tradition. We understand John's position by going back into Israel's history and rediscovering the two strands of Messianic prediction. In one, salvation for Israel was to come in the form of an earthly Messiah who would bring, peace, protection, and prosperity to God's people.[98]

In contrast, apocalyptic eschatology saw the world as too evil to be saved. The present age must pass away to prepare for a new heaven and a new earth.[99] From this perspective, the Messiah is not only an historical person but also a transcendent figure, bringing salvation from God. The final kingdom does not grow out of this world and its history, but rather breaks into it. There are two ages: this age, and the age to come.

The Defeat of Gog and Magog (Revelation 20:1-6)

John announced previously that Satan, after being bound for a thousand years, must be released for a while (20:3). We naturally wonder why. The answer is for literary and theological reasons. John has yet another picture to include as part of the final defeat of Satan. The Gog and Magog story of Ezekiel 38-39 needs to be inserted, since John is following the Ezekiel story.

---

[98] Ezekiel 34:25-31

[99] Isaiah 65:17; 66:22; 2 Peter 3:12-13

Ezekiel painted a graphic picture of "Gog, of the land of Magog, the chief prince of Meshech and Tubal" whom God would raise up in the last days as the epitome of evil to attack Israel with a great host. God would then destroy him and his armies to demonstrate His sovereignty. For Ezekiel, Gog is a foil to show God's power.[100]

By John's time, Jewish tradition had transformed the story into "Gog and Magog" and made them together into a symbol of the ultimate enemy. To fulfill this mythical prophecy, the devil must be released to once more deceive the nations so that they rise up against God's people. But fire quickly falls from heaven and consumes this last army. The devil is finally thrown into the pit of fire and sulfur to join the Beast and the false prophet, all of whom are to be tormented day and night forever.

The Meaning and Message for Us

Now I want to set the doctrine of the second coming of Christ into a larger framework. In a sense the term "second coming of Christ" is too limiting. He came at the time of the creation of the earth, because all things were made through him (John 1:3). He came in the manger at Bethlehem. He came back from the dead at the resurrection. He came in the power of the Holy Spirit at Pentecost. But there is, in addition, a promised final return of the Lord. Christians look back upon the life, death, and resurrection of Christ with awe and

---

100 Ezekiel 38:16, 23; 39:7-13

gratitude. We look forward to a final consummation of history and the final victory of Christ.

From my perspective, some distort the gospel and build most of their thinking around the "second coming of Christ." They speculate on details and argue about them. They try to prove various time schedules from the book of Revelation. This is not a new fad. In every generation there have been those who have tried to predict the date and circumstances of Christ's return. The number of such prophets increases in times of widespread tension and despair, when hope for earthly peace and justice seems far away.

Today when a preacher announces that he will explain the time and manner of the "Second Coming," crowds of curious and gullible people throng to the meeting. However, the revelation of Christ's second coming was given not to satisfy our curiosity but to strengthen us in our struggle. When we envision "the kingdom of God" coming on earth as in heaven and work to support opportunity for the poor and oppressed, we are working for this return. We are not doing the will of Christ if we sit back and speculate about his return. The New Testament emphasized the practical value of this doctrine for daily living. We know that we face a defeated enemy and follow a victorious Christ. We can endure the injustices and defeats of life because we know these are temporary. The vision of the victorious living Christ helps us to live courageously and to witness with full assurance.

Timing of Christ's Return

When will Christ return? The disciples wanted an answer. During his last appearance after the resurrection they asked Jesus, "'Lord, is this the time when you will restore the kingdom to Israel?' He replied, 'It is not for you to know times or periods that the Father has set by his own authority.'" Rather than waste time speculating about when he would return, Jesus said, "'But you will receive power when the Holy Spirit has come upon you; and you will be my witnesses in Jerusalem, in all Judea and Samaria, and to the ends of the earth.'"[101]

Most Christians in the New Testament era, including those living when Revelation was written, expected Christ's return in their own lifetime. The earliest Christians were shocked when some of their number died before Christ came again. Paul wrote about the resurrection to give assurance that even after death the Christians will be included in this wondrous return. John, the writer of Revelation, obviously expected the Second Coming with the overthrow of the Roman Emperor, Domitian. But Jesus had said, "It is not for you to know times or periods…." (Acts 1:7)

Premillennial and Postmillennial Perspectives

The entire New Testament teaches that Christ will come again. The question remains: will the world be brought into his fold before that time, or will evil continue to prevail until that hour? Will a sisterhood

---

[101] Acts 1:6-8

and brotherhood of humanity come to bow at the feet of Jesus, or will humanity shatter history and destroy the earth as Christ returns? Generally, the "premillennial" perspective is that the forces of evil are too strong to allow for the kingdom of God to be realized on earth before the second coming of Christ. The "postmillennial" perspective is that the world can be brought increasingly into alignment with God's will through the diligent efforts of the faithful who work under God's guidance to bring love and justice into the world. Both the pre- and postmillennialists have Biblical truths to share with us. We would be poorer without either of their insights.

Those who hold that the world cannot be redeemed in history know the tenacious grip that sin has on life. There has been a heightening of goodness in our day, but with each advance new problems have been created. Evil has become more refined and powerful. Only when the scroll of time has been rolled up can absolute peace and goodness reign.

Yet there is truth in the other position. Is there not the promise in the New Testament that Christ will rule all things? The great missionary hymns express the Biblical hope that the world will be won to Christ. "The earth shall be full of His knowledge and glory, as waters that cover the seas!" "Jesus shall reign where're the sun doth his successive journeys run." This is not a naïve idealism tied to the gospel. It is not a theory of evolutionary progress with a Galilean accent. It is the gospel. Who can place a limit on the reach and penetration of sacrificial love? Jesus said, "And I, when

I am lifted up from the earth, will draw all men to myself."[102]

At this point in the discussion, it is appropriate for us to consider the issue of multiculturalism. For God's kingdom to come on earth, must everyone be converted to Christianity in the traditional sense? All of the world's great religions and spiritual traditions aspire to the realization of human life in its highest potential. Each sees humans as being made in the image of God in some sense. Each seeks to harmonize heaven and earth, even though this essential aspiration may be expressed in slightly different terms, and different traditions might have different ideas about how this can be achieved. Indeed, other traditions, as well as Christianity, have this tension between a vision that this kind of perfection can be brought about and lived among human beings on earth and the other belief that this perfection can only exist on a transcendental or heavenly level.

Christ in a universal, essential sense represents the Divine expressed in human form. The Church as the Body of Christ in a universal sense may extend beyond the traditional idea of the Christian Church to represent the entire human community being able to live on earth in truth, peace, and harmony. God works in mysterious ways. It is inappropriately limiting to think that God only works through the Christian church. At the same time, this more universal appreciation and

---

[102] John 12:32

perspective need not dilute our own devotion to Jesus Christ or our Christian commitment to working through our churches and in our lives to bring the kingdom of God on earth.

Those who feel the world cannot be redeemed – either in the traditional sense that not everyone will convert to Christianity or in the more universal sense that evil can never be completely stamped out – remind us that always there will be wars and rumors of wars. They point to the parable of "the wheat and the tares," in which the tares grow among the wheat. The master of the farm says to let them grow together until the harvest. "...At harvest time I will tell the reapers, 'Collect the weeds first and bind them in bundles to be burned, but gather the wheat into my barn.'"[103]

The postmillennialists who see a redeemed world remind us that Christ will put all things under his feet.[104] The apostle Paul wrote that Christ will unite all things in himself, "things in heaven and things on earth."[105] The angels of Revelation sing, "The kingdom of the world has become the kingdom of our Lord and of his Messiah...." (11:15)

Premillennialists remind us of the power of evil. They protect us from a soft optimism that sees the future through rose-colored glasses. They remind us of the constant struggle that must be ours in working for the

---

[103] Matthew 13:24-30

[104] Ephesians 1:22

[105] Ephesians 1:10

will of God. The postmillennialists, on the other hand, emphasize the power of God to redeem and God's relentless love for His/Her creation that will not rest until every tear is wiped from every eye. By giving us hope they spur us on to fight the evil around us. They call on us to make real the words of the Lord's Prayer: "Your kingdom come. Your will be done on earth as it is in heaven." They keep us from the pessimism of despair that would cause us to sit down and wait for a future kingdom instead of acting to build God's kingdom now.

Christ's Return Related to Our Response

At this time in history, humanity has access to immense destructive power. Our nuclear, biological, or chemical weapons have the potential to destroy life on earth. Our corporate greed and widespread addiction to unsustainable ways of living are causing unprecedented environmental degradation—deforestation, falling water tables, desertification, species extinctions, pollution of the oceans, global warming—that threatens the earth's ability to support life as we know it. Could God allow humanity to bring its own history to an end in one or more of these ways?

Conversely, the unprecedented scientific developments of our age could turn the deserts of the world into gardens of plenty. The rays of the sun can be captured and harnessed to provide us with energy. The earth's resources could be managed responsibly and sustainably for the benefit of all, if Christian values of love and justice were developed to keep pace with the technological developments. It is not necessary for people to suffer from a lack of the physical necessities of life or to fight with neighbors over scarce resources.

Our world has been shrinking in size like a balloon as the air is let out. Air travel makes it possible to fly in the rising sun from London to New York. A voice transmitted by radio is heard on the opposite side of the earth sooner than it is heard in the back of the auditorium where the words are spoken. Anybody with a cell phone can easily talk to almost anyone else almost anywhere on earth. The computer and the internet have bound common people together in a communication network that makes us world neighbors in fact, each with the cumulative knowledge and information of humanity at our fingertips. We live in the back yard of the world.

Today the instruments are in hand to destroy the earth according to the predictions of the premillennialists. Yet we also have the means and ability, with God's grace, to lead the world into a blessed community as envisaged by the postmillennialists. It is possible, through God's Spirit, to make our world neighborhood into the kingdom of God!

The critical message is that, with the enormous problems facing the world now, the necessity for "repentance" is becoming increasingly obvious and urgent. With our ever increasing technology and expanding knowledge we are forced to choose between building this common community and reaping the results of a final catastrophe. What a gigantic challenge faces us all! From the perspective of the Christian faith, what a challenge faces the churches! How much we need to throw off our lethargy and our small plans and truly dedicate our imaginations and our resources to building a just and peaceful world community based on the message and spirit of Christ!

The Bible intentionally leaves unanswered the question of the timing and the exact nature of the End, while indicating that our input counts in God's plan. Is it too much to hope that our zeal will hasten the establishment of God's kingdom everywhere?

Questions for Discussion

1. What is your understanding of angels?
2. Can you see spiritual truth in each of the seven visions of the "second coming?"
3. Can the world become a garden of plenty and a place where all people have the opportunity to reach their human potential?
4. Do you have a vision of goodness prevailing ultimately? Or, is the premillennial assertion more likely, that the world ends in disaster?
5. Do you believe that everyone must convert to Christianity in order for God's kingdom to come on earth?
6. Do you have a belief in the reign of God at the end of history, even if we cannot express or explain exactly what it will be like?

Chapter 12

THE LAST JUDGMENT

and

THE BOOK OF LIFE OPENED

Revelation 20:11-15

A farmer posted a "No Trespassing" sign to keep neighborhood boys from crossing his property. One embittered youth decided to get even. One night he slipped onto the farm with a sack of Johnson grass seed and sowed it generously in several fields. (Johnson grass is a weed that spreads rapidly and is hard to destroy.) A few years later the boy married this farmer's only daughter. A short time later the old man died, and this same boy inherited the farm. He spent the next several years fighting Johnson grass.

There seems to be a law of sowing and reaping. When we sow to the wind we reap the whirlwind. We cast love and caring upon the waters of life, and like the tide that comes in, these return to us with an abundance of joy.

Nevertheless, life is never completely fair. Jesus noted that the rain falls on both the just and the unjust. Often the wicked prosper at the expense of the righteous. The writer of Revelation felt that a judgment beyond this life is necessary if the books are to be balanced and if justice is to finally prevail.

The thieves who robbed and stole on the Jericho road got rich and retired to the suburbs of Jerusalem. There they were honored because of their wealth. If the courts questioned their past connection with the underworld, they employed the best lawyers and bought off witnesses. Conversely, the innocent people who were beaten and robbed were maimed for life. As cripples they could no longer work; they were relegated to lives of pain and poverty.

Is real justice written into the DNA of our experience? The book of Revelation says "yes" because we are citizens of two worlds. There is a justice beyond the courts of earth. God is on the great white throne. A symbolic Book of Life in heaven will be opened some day.

The Last Judgment

The book of Revelation has drawn on other biblical imagery in depicting an ultimate evil power in the person of Satan, the serpent. The Devil goes up and down the earth seeking those whom he may destroy. But in the end Satan is thrown into a pit that is sealed. He gets loose after a thousand years, but then is cast into outer darkness forever.

If earth is to become free for human fulfillment, then all that destroys life must be destroyed. But the reign of Satan was always a paradox. Our sinning is, in one sense, the result of Satan's power – forces beyond our control. Nonetheless, we can and must resist sin. We are responsible for our own moral conduct. The fact that Satan is loose and active does not excuse our wrongdoing.

Once more we are transported to heaven where John sees a "...great white throne and the one who sat on it...." (20:11) Again and again, John has brought us to the brink of a final judgment. Now we are actually there. The scene is brief and terse. The universal judgment of the dead is about to begin. Not only are nations and rulers called to account for their deeds, but also every individual faces an hour in which he or she must submit to the final judgment of God.

John sees the heavenly throne and the One who is seated on it. Throughout biblical literature, humans never actually see God. They see a whirlwind or a burning bush. John saw the throne of God many times and heard the voice of one speaking from the throne, but it was always assumed that no person could see God and live. Now God reveals Himself to John.

The throne has been a central focus of this revelation. Here, as elsewhere, it has a political connotation. The throne of the dragon and the beast[106] issues decrees and judgments that determine the earthly

---

[106] Revelation 13:2

fate of the Christian community. Roman courts often condemn Christians who are faithful. Now all of those court verdicts are appealed to a higher court. Caesar may control the courts of justice in his empire, but there is a final judge who is not arbitrary or capricious.

"And the sea gave up the dead that were in it, Death and Hades gave up the dead that were in them, and all were judged according to what they had done." (20:13) When the book of deeds is opened, the accounts will be made to balance. Every damnable deed of persecution will be punished. Every response of love and forgiveness will have its reward. God is absolutely serious about our responsibility to act honestly and fairly. In our freedom we are judged by what we do. And what we do not only matters; it matters ultimately.

We learn that the sea gave up its dead. Israelites placed great importance on the place of burial. Those who perished at sea were considered to be especially unfortunate because there was no burial site for the body to await the resurrection. But even those without graves are included.

Two different books serve as the basis for judgment. In one are recorded the good deeds and the failures of every human being (20: 12). In the other, the "book of life," are written the names of those who have been chosen for salvation.[107] The first judgment is based on the person's deeds. The second judgment, having one's name written in the Lamb's book of life, is

---

107 Philippians 2:12-13; Luke 10:20; Hebrews 12:23

based on one's confession of faith and steadfast testimony. This is not dependent on our achievements, but on God's grace.

The two judgments are pictured in the same scene, yet they are very different. They comprise the paradox of works and faith with which Paul and James wrestled. In the Pauline tradition we are saved by grace through faith.[108] But for James, faith without works is dead.[109] Just as we are ultimately responsible for what we do, so God is ultimately responsible for our salvation. John portrays both.

In the first judgment, all are judged. This is no self-serving portrayal in which the Christians are protected from the results of their actions. Christians and pagans alike are judged, based on what they have done. Rulers and great nations may be judged more harshly than a lowly person. Judgment is fair and impartial, as we shall see.

Jesus' Teachings on Judgment

Jesus said: "When the Son of man comes in his glory, and all the angels with him, then he will sit on the throne of his glory. All the nations will be gathered before him, and he will separate people one from another as a shepherd separates the sheep from the goats, and he will put the sheep at his right hand and the goats at the left. Then the king will say to those at his

---

108 Ephesians 2:8-10

109 James 2:14-17

right hand, 'Come, you that are blessed by my Father, inherit the kingdom prepared for you from the foundation of the world; for I was hungry and you gave me food, I was thirsty, and you gave me something to drink, I was a stranger and you welcomed me, I was naked and you gave me clothing, I was sick and you took care of me, I was in prison and you visited me.' Then the righteous will answer him, 'Lord, when was it that we saw you hungry and gave you food, or thirsty and gave you something to drink? And when was it that we saw you a stranger and welcomed you, or naked and gave you clothing? And when was it that we saw you sick or in prison and visited you?' And the king will answer them, 'Truly, I tell you, just as you did it to one of the least of these who are members of my family, you did it to me.'"[110]

Those words of Jesus reveal that we are judged on the basis of what we have done, most especially on behalf of the weak and the vulnerable. In the scripture passage from Revelation we find the same truth. "...And the dead were judged according to their works, as recorded in the books." (20:12)

This I Believe

This is a strange judgment. Jesus identified himself with the sick, blind, imprisoned, hungry, thirsty and cold. These are the people about whom Christ is supremely concerned. When we help such persons we help him. In that final judgment the important thing is

---

[110] Matthew 25:31-40

not, "Were you a Catholic or a Baptist or a Methodist?" The real question will be, "Did you have Christ living in your life, and did you express that Presence by caring about those for whom Jesus expressed his supreme concern?"

Again, we are dealing with symbols. This is not a literal book. God does not actually instruct a recording angel to take pen and ink and write down every thought and deed. The story says imaginatively that the all-wise and all-knowing God keeps in His understanding all that has been done. God knows all about us. We are judged both by our deeds and by our love for God.

Limited vs. Universal Salvation

"Then Death and Hades were thrown into the lake of fire. This is the second death, the lake of fire; and anyone whose name was not found written in the book of life was thrown into the lake of fire." (20:14-15)

Evidence that this is symbolic language is the claim that Death and Hades are also thrown into the burning lake. Here is the symbolic promise that death will be destroyed, that we will live forever. In our world, all of life continues by devouring other forms of life. Now, in this vision, the Giver of life finally destroys predatory life and death.[111]

But what do we make of the statement that Hades is also cast into the lake of fire? Does God ultimately

---

[111] Isaiah 11:6-9

destroy hell itself? I turn now to discuss a central question about the end of history and the culmination of God's kingdom for humanity: belief in limited salvation versus belief in universal salvation.

At first it seems absurd to suppose that John supported salvation for all creation. The book contains so many passages that seem to reveal a vindictive spirit. This leads many people to reject the book as scripture. One can interpret eternal damnation as the just consequence for those who reject the call of Christ and make the argument that God is not vindictive when opportunity for salvation has been provided but not accepted. A more careful study of this issue is important for our larger understanding of God's nature and purpose.

Salvation implies a blessed quality of life, as we experience the presence of God, love God, and serve others. Universal salvation means that all human beings will ultimately know this salvation because of God's unconditional grace manifest in Jesus Christ. Limited salvation, by contrast, is the view that only those who come to Christ prior to their death will enjoy eternal life with God, while all others are cast into the lake of fire to live there in torture forever.

These terms, "limited" or "universal" salvation, are not found in the book of Revelation or in the New Testament. In fact, the author of Revelation never used the verb "save" or the noun "savior." He only used the world "salvation" three times, and never to denote the final destiny of persons. Each time it was used as praise to God, "…Salvation belongs to our God who is seated upon the throne, and to the Lamb." (7:10) (See also 12:10 and 19:1.) But John does offer imaginative pictures of both universal and limited salvation.

Many texts in Revelation can be understood to portray or imply universal salvation: "Then I heard every creature in heaven and on earth and under the earth and in the sea, and all that is in them, singing, 'To the one seated on the throne and to the Lamb be blessing and honor and glory and might forever and ever!'" (5:13) Or this passage: "All nations will come and worship before you, for your judgments have been revealed." (15:4b) We shall find shortly in Chapter 21:24-27 that the gates to the heavenly city will never be shut, implying that they are open eternally to welcome all those who wish to enter.

Other texts indicate a limited salvation, including the passage (21:10-15) concerning the twelve gates of the new Jerusalem being inscribed with the names of the twelve tribes of Israel and the twelve foundations being inscribed with the names of the twelve apostles. To take another example, "Then another angel, a third, followed them, crying with a loud voice, 'Those who worship the beast and its image, and receive a mark on their foreheads or on their hands, they will also drink the wine of God's wrath, poured unmixed into the cup of his anger, and they will be tormented with fire and sulfur in the presence of the holy angels and in the presence of the Lamb. And the smoke of their torment goes up forever and ever....'" (14:9-11a)

This same paradox exists in other parts of the Bible. Verses that connote limited salvation include

Isaiah 26:21; Matthew 25:31-46; John 3:16; John 3:36 and 2 Thessalonians 1:6-9. In the parable in Matthew Jesus concludes, "And they will go away into eternal punishment, but the righteous into eternal life." John 3:36 records Jesus' words again: "Whoever believes in the Son has eternal life; whoever disobeys the Son will not see life, but must endure God's wrath."

Another theological strand is explicitly inclusive, implying a universal salvation. The Psalmist wrote (Psalm 86:9), "All the nations you have made shall come and bow before you, O Lord, and shall glorify your name." Or note the words of Isaiah (Isaiah 45:22-23), "Turn to me and be saved, all the ends of the earth! For I am God, and there is no other.... To me every knee shall bow, every tongue shall swear."

In John's gospel Jesus is quoted as saying, "And I, when I am lifted up from the earth, will draw all people to myself." (John 12:32) Or again, "Indeed, God did not send the Son into the world to condemn the world, but in order that the world might be saved through him." (John 3:17)

The apostle Paul expressed this theme of universal salvation in almost every one of his epistles. "There just as one man's trespass led to condemnation for all, so one man's act of righteousness leads to justification and life for all men." (Romans 5:18) Also, Paul wrote to the Romans, "For God has imprisoned all in disobedience, so that he may be merciful to all." (Romans 11:32-33) Again Paul wrote, "...that God may be all in all." (1 Corinthians 15:27-28) Or, in any one of many passages in Ephesians, "For he has made known with all wisdom and insight the mystery of his will, according to his good pleasure he set forth in Christ as a plan for the fullness of time, to gather up all things in him, things in heaven and things on earth." (Ephesians 1:9-10) Again, "that at the name of Jesus every knee should bend, in heaven and on earth and under the earth, and every tongue should confess that Jesus Christ is Lord, to the glory of God the Father." (Philippians 2:10-11) Three final examples from Paul: "For in him all the fullness of God was pleased to dwell, and through him to reconcile to himself all things, whether on earth or in heaven, making peace by the blood of the cross." (Colossians 1:18-20) "For to this end we toil and struggle, because we have our hope set on the living God, who is the Savior of all people, especially of those who believe." (I Timothy 4:10) "For the grace of God has appeared, bringing salvation to all." (Titus 2:11)

Resolving the Paradox

There are three distinct approaches we can take to resolving this paradox. First, we can accept the concept of universal salvation, believing it is the dominant theme, and then interpret limited salvation passages in a figurative way. Second, we can do the opposite and accept the concept of limited salvation, believing it is the dominant theme, and then interpret universal salvation passages in a figurative way. Third, we can say that John and other writers do not have a single consistent view but present multiple perspectives. For a logical treatise, such inconsistency would be a weakness. But with the use of vivid imagery and the tension created by the paradoxical perspectives, the scriptures can create a powerful experience of the incomprehensible mystery, majesty and greatness of God.

This I Believe

There are several themes that must be stated and preserved in my quest for deeper truth. First, I believe Jesus revealed a God who is love, who, like the good shepherd, searches for the lost sheep until He finds it and returns it to the fold. This is God's nature. Second, human beings must be free to choose their course and accept or reject God's love. Third, people are responsible for their decisions and actions, and we are all affected by the consequences of our choices. We must never trivialize the deadly conflict between good and evil. Fourth, God hates sin because it separates us from Him, but God loves sinners and wills that all be brought into fellowship with Him.

Through years of searching and, I hope, growth, I have come to believe in universal salvation. The strongest and most lasting reality in the universe is the unending, searching love of God for all who are estranged. This I believe.

Limited salvation points to the urgency of getting life on the right track now. "...See, now is the day of salvation!" (2 Corinthians 6:2) We do not have a day to lose or waste. Those who believe in universal salvation agree that so long as people have life and breath they can choose new life. If their background is in the context of the Christian faith, they can choose new life in Christ. But they also believe that the opportunity for this choice never ends. Hell is separation from God; heaven is life with God. When a person in this life or in the life beyond hears the compassionate call of God and responds, that person moves to God's presence and hence into heaven. Those who believe in universal salvation believe that the love of God is so great that finally all people will respond and be saved. We can affirm this conviction while still asserting God's judgment on sin, which separates people from each other and all of us from God.[112]

The Course Completed

Look at our act of commitment to Christ as our entrance into his school. From this point of view, Christ becomes our teacher, the Church is our classroom, the Bible is our principal textbook, the world is our laboratory and fellow Christians are classmates.

Many people have the mistaken idea that to enroll in the class, to accept Christ as Savior and join the church is all there is to the course. They feel it is sufficient to have their names on the roll book. No, that is not the end; it is just the beginning.

I remember my first day of school. My mother went with me. The teacher asked my name, and I almost forgot it. I was enrolled in school! But that was just the beginning, not the end. I went through the first grade, the second, and on to advanced study.

---

[112] Harrington, Wilfred, *Revelation, Proclaiming a Vision of Hope,* pp. 37-46. See also Boring, M. Eugene, ***op. cit.***, pp. 226-231.

When your name is written in the Lamb's book of life, it is the beginning of a journey that never ends. Christian growth, service and worship can last for a lifetime; growth and service continue forever, even after entering the portals of heaven.

The whole book of Revelation makes it clear that the standards are high and the study is difficult, but the person who finishes the course reaps the rewards: the joy of knowing God, the peace and joy of loving other persons, and the challenges involved in working for justice for "the least of these."

Some cloudless morning, commencement will come. We close our eyes for the last time as our eternal spirits leave our bodies at death. Then we hear a graduation march. We find ourselves walking down the aisle in step with the music of a heavenly chorus. We take the seats reserved for us. Christ delivers the commencement address. I hear him say, "Well done, good and trustworthy slave; ...enter into the joy of your master." (Matthew 25:23) The Lamb's book of life is opened. God calls your name. You stand, receive your diploma, and enter the company of those who have met the requirements for graduation. As our class leaves the stage, we change the tassel from left to right. Our black robes are changed into spotless robes of white, as together we sing the praises of our Alma Mater, the God of all creation.

Postscript: A Biblical Perspective on Hell

The words, "Death and Hades gave up the dead in them" offers us an opportunity to reflect on a Biblical understanding of Hades or hell.[113] Hell is the word generally used by translators for the Hebrew word "Sheol." But many passages in the Hebrew scripture using Sheol simply mean "the grave." It is deep (Job 11:8) and dark (Job 12:22). It is fastened with gates (Isaiah 38:10, 17) and bars (Job 17:16). In this underworld are the souls of the dead. It is clear that in many Old Testament passages Sheol can only mean "the grave." (See also Genesis 37:35 and 1 Samuel 2:6.)

But in other passages Sheol seems to involve the notion of punishment and is translated as "hell" (Psalm 86:13; Psalm 89:48; Proverbs 23:14).

In the New Testament, the word "Hades," like Sheol, sometimes means merely "the grave," as it does in Revelation 20:13 or in Acts 2:31.

The Christian creed says of Jesus after his death on the cross, "He descended into hell" (Hades), meaning the state of the dead without any connotation of happiness or misery (Ephesians 4:9; Acts 2:25-29). This is similar to the meaning of Hades in Greek mythology, a place inhabited by the spirits of the dead.

Elsewhere in the New Testament, the word "Hades" is a place of torment (Luke 16:23; 2 Peter 2:4; Matthew 11:23-24).

Consequently, in Roman Catholic doctrine, Hades is understood as an intermediate state between

---

113 In this postscript, I place the large number of biblical references in the text rather than in footnotes, so that the reader may more easily access the references, if desired.

death and resurrection, divided into two parts—one an abode of the "Saved" and the other the dwelling place of the "Lost." Much of this theology is based on Jesus' parable of Dives, the wealthy man who went to hell because of his lack of compassion for the poor and Lazarus, the beggar refused by Dives who went to heaven. But a parable is a story with a heavenly meaning. It was not meant by Jesus to be taken literally. To ground a doctrine on the imagery of a parable is dangerous theology.

The Hebrew word for hell is "Hinnom" which became "Gehinnon" or "Gehenna" to denote a place of torment. Jesus used the term in Matthew 5:29, 10:28, and 23:15. It is recorded also In Mark 9:43 and Luke 12:5.

The valley of Hinnom is a deep narrow ravine with steep rocky sides, located south and west of Jerusalem. The earliest mention of the valley of Hinnom is in Joshua 15:8 and 18:16. The boundary between the tribes of Judah and Benjamin is described as passing along the bed of this ravine. It became a dumping ground where refuse was burned. Ahaz and Manasseh made their child "pass through the fire" in this valley (2 Kings 16:3), and the custom of infant sacrifice to fire gods was practiced for a considerable period at Topheth—at the southeast end of the valley. (Jeremiah 7:31) To put an end to this evil practice King Josiah rendered the area ceremonially unclean by spreading human bones over the area. (2 Kings 23:10-14) From this foul burning and unclean ground came the Hebrew image of hell as a place of fire.

Questions for Discussion

1. Do you understand the need for a final judgment to "balance the books" against injustice on earth? Is that important?
2. How do you react to Jesus' criteria for judgment, that "...as you did it to one of the least of these my brethren, you did it to me?" Do you agree with me that this is a strange judgment?
3. My discussion of "limited" versus "universal" salvation is one of the most controversial positions I hold and is strongly rejected by many. Do you feel that I adequately account for human sinfulness and people's rejection of God's love? Can people be in hell for a time but not forever? How long does the "Good Shepherd" keep searching for the lost sheep?
4. What is your concept of hell?

Chapter 13

THE NEW JERUSALEM
Revelation 21, 22

In these final chapters of Revelation, John brings to an end his sweeping saga of victory. But before the curtain descends on this epic drama, there is a final scene that reveals the Church triumphant. The old order has passed away. We soar in spirit to the portals of a New Jerusalem and sense the joy of living forever with God in the company of the redeemed.

A New Heaven and a New Earth (Revelation 21:1-8)

"And I saw the holy city, the new Jerusalem, coming down out of heaven from God, prepared as a bride adorned for her husband." (21:2) The passage is taken from Isaiah 65:17-19. This city was not built by human engineers and craftsmen; it is God's gift to us and appears to be located on earth. The union between God and humanity is consummated. This marriage will never end in divorce; it will last forever.

The old Jerusalem, center of Israel's life, was mixed in its receptivity to Jesus and his teachings, though virtually all of the early Christians were Jews. The New Jerusalem is a place of grace and joy where the sacred community draws its life from Jesus, the Christ. Now there is intimate communion between God and His people, a vision glimpsed and hoped for by ancient prophets.[114] Before giving a positive description of life in the new city, John tells us what it is not. We learn that it is not a place where we experience sin and death. They have been destroyed. There is neither sorrow nor crying, because "... the former things have passed away." (21:4) Then God speaks for almost the last time in the book, "...See, I am making all things new...." (21:5) God confirms the prophetic promise of Isaiah[115] and Paul's declaration that all things will be made new.[116]

At the beginning of Revelation God is revealed as "Alpha and Omega," the beginning and the ending of all things. Now we are at the end, and it turns out to be a new beginning. Once more John turns his attention from heaven to the churches (21:7-8) with the message that has been consistent since Chapter 2:10b: "Be faithful until death, and I will give you the crown of life." The faithless, those whose lives are "polluted," will not share this treasure. Those Christians who are tempted to backslide or desert the faith and worship Caesar rather than Christ are asked to consider the magnitude of the promised benefits for remaining faithful.

---

114 Ezekiel 37:27; Zechariah 2:10-12

115 Isaiah 65:17-19

116 1 Corinthians 13:9-10

Spread before us is the glory of this new city. There are four facets to the sparkling splendor of heaven: perfect security; perfect fellowship; provision for every need; and finally, constant opportunity to serve God.

A Secure City (Revelation 21:9-21)

I imagine those early Christians became jubilant as they read of the protection provided in the Holy City. "God is the light." There will be no darkness where evil deeds can flourish. The New Jerusalem is surrounded by a wall, symbol of security in the ancient world. There are twelve gates to the city, reminding us that the inhabitants will come from all parts of the world. The names of the twelve tribes of Israel are written on the gates. The people of Israel will be admitted, as the fulfillment of God's longstanding covenant with the Hebrew people. Indeed, the book of Revelation makes clear at many points that the Hebrew people are integral members of the company of heaven. Their religious symbols are used throughout. It is their "New Jerusalem." The 24 elders before the throne are representatives of the twelve tribes of Israel and the twelve disciples. The Church is seen as the culmination of God's covenant with the Hebrew people.

Under the walls of the city are twelve foundations on which are inscribed the names of the twelve disciples of Jesus. Walls built on such firm foundations can never be shaken or battered down. Peter had once confessed to Jesus, "'You are the Messiah, the Son of the living God.' And Jesus answered him, 'Blessed are you.... For flesh and blood has not revealed this to you, but my Father in heaven. And I tell you, you are Peter, and on this rock I will build my church....'"[117]

Next we read that the city is measured (21:15ff). "The city lies foursquare," symbolizing its perfection. The breadth, length, height and depth measure twelve thousand furlongs. Remember that in Revelation all numbers are used as symbols. Twelve thousand is twelve times ten times ten. From these numbers we understand that the city is both perfect and complete. There is no point in using our calculators to compute how many people could fit into a city of fifteen hundred miles square. The walls are long enough to enclose all of the redeemed.

In addition to the stunning architecture, the adornments are beyond imagination. The streets are paved with pure gold. Beautiful jewels adorn the city walls. The precious jewels correspond to those found on the breastplate of the high priest of Israel, where each jewel represents one of the twelve tribes of Israel.[118] Priestly splendor is appropriate in the abode of Christians who on earth took the role of priests, ministering in the name of Christ. The twelve gates are made from twelve beautiful pearls (21:21). After all, Christians had renounced all lesser jewels to obtain

---

117 Matthew 16:16-18; 1 Corinthians 3:10; Ephesians 2:20

118 Exodus 28:17-21

Christ, the "one pearl of great value."[119] John paints visual images of these most precious stones to convey the harmonious richness and beauty of the city.

A Perfect Fellowship (Revelation 21:22-27)

Next, this new home of the saints is portrayed as a place of perfect fellowship. God will dwell with us. There is no need for a special tabernacle where people go to meet God, because the entire city is one great church. In this city God and the Lamb are present for everyone. The immediate presence of God, already experienced through the Holy Spirit, is affirmed and completed (21:22).

The nations of the world come to present their gifts, not literally, but as metaphor of the universal community bowing to Christ. This great fellowship is free from distance and free from the fear of hostile nations. Further, the communion of heaven is not complicated by class structures and struggles; all humans live together in the light of God's presence. (21:24)

This I Believe

In the rich experience of church fellowship we have a foretaste of heaven. I have witnessed the light of new truth shining on the face of a church member who has participated in group discussion of a doctrine of the faith. I have seen the shared excitement when Christians accept the challenge of some great task. I

---

[119] Matthew 13:45-46

have sensed the joy of the person who has introduced another to Christ. I have observed the firm handshake of hearty congratulation for a moral victory won. I have witnessed the strong arm of sympathy on the shoulder of a friend in an hour of bereavement. Such fellowship makes any church "an outpost of heaven."

Provision for Every Need (Revelation 22:1-2)

John then turns our attention from the wonderful fellowship of the city to the abundant provision for all our needs as residents. The "river of the water of life" issues from the throne of God, with the "the tree of life" on its banks. The tree multiplies into a great orchard and these trees bear fruit every month, "...and the leaves of the tree are for the healing of the nations." (22:2)

Sparkling water, abundant food and medical herbs are lavishly provided for the residents. The scene, again, has its origins with Ezekiel.[120] During the Babylonian captivity this prophet of God saw a miraculous river flowing from the temple at Jerusalem to the Dead Sea, irrigating the desert along its banks. The living water turned that stagnant sea into a pure beautiful lake. (Then, as now, no trees grew on the banks of the Dead Sea; there were no fish in the waters; even birds would not fly over it.) Ezekiel saw fruit ripening on richly laden trees where previously nothing had grown. Moreover, a new crop of fruit could be

---

[120] Ezekiel 47:1-12

harvested every month, and the leaves could be used for healing.

For the Jews in captivity, this was a pledge of restored favor with God after they returned to their homes in Jerusalem. John took this imagery and applied it to the New Jerusalem, with the river flowing from God's throne. This river ran alongside the major boulevard, with trees growing in a park along the banks.

"Nothing accursed will be found there any more…." (22:3) Adam and Eve were driven from the Garden of Eden under the spell of a curse. Sin entered the human family and marred the image of God within each of us. Now the curse is broken forever. In Genesis we have the story of "paradise lost." At the close of the Bible is the story of "paradise regained." The first paradise was portrayed as a garden; the last paradise is a restored garden. The "tree of the knowledge of good and evil" in Eden was the occasion for the curse,[121] and the curse involved no longer having access to the tree of life. Now, at the fulfillment of time, God's people once again live in a beautiful garden with the tree of life, and the trees spread in profusion as an orchard in the midst of this paradise.

Worship and Service (Revelation 22:3-5)

We have found the New Jerusalem to be a place of security, community and abundant provision. Now we come to understand heaven as a place for positive worship and service. The city has no temple; only a

---

[121] Genesis 2:9-17; 3:22-24

throne. It is a single throne shared by God and the Lamb (22:3). Paul had written, "but we preach Christ crucified,...Christ the power of God and the wisdom of God."[122] "...And his servants will worship him." (22:3) In contrast to this translation from the New Revised Standard Version, the King James text says, "And his servants shall serve him." The distinction is lost between worship and service; the two become one. When we worship God we serve Him. The reverse is also true. Our service to Him is our act of devotion.

Heaven is not a place of idleness but of service. This should make us pause and reexamine our attitude toward serving Christ. He who begrudges Christian worship and service on earth will have a great deal of growing to do before enjoying eternity serving God. Conversely, those who find their supreme joy in Christian service are thrilled by the words, "His servants shall serve him."

Heaven is often pictured as a place of rest. This portrait is drawn from the experience of overworked persons whose highest pleasure was to find moments of rest and relaxation. But the "rest" of heaven does not mean that we sit down and go to sleep. It does not mean that we retire from active duty. It is not the rest of the aged or the ill. The rest of heaven means that we shall have purified powers for greater service. We are free from weariness. Ours is a rest from sin, making us

---

[122] 1 Corinthians 1:23-24

more awake and alive. We are invigorated for all the activities of heaven.

"And they will see his face...." (22:4) Christians who have lived by faith want to see God face to face. Too long we have seen through a mirror dimly.[123] In that Holy City we shall stand in his near presence and look into his radiant, loving face.

"And they will reign forever and ever." (22:5b) Like a great symphony with a central theme and many sub-themes, the central vision of the book is restated once again. We have experienced a multitude of images designed to convey that Christ, not Caesar, is triumphant and to reveal the beauty and joy of life with God. Now we come back to the central theme of light and to the center of paradise, the throne of God and the Lamb. We join the great company of heaven in sharing the reign of God "forever and ever."

We have come to the end of John's visions in Revelation.

The Epilogue (Revelation 22:6-21)

These verses, first, form a bridge back to the preface (1:1-3). Second, they make clear that Jesus is the true author; nothing in the book is to be changed by anyone. Third, the epilogue is designed to help the churches appropriate the message. Finally, it provides language for use in the Eucharist of that early church.

---

[123] 1 Corinthians 13:12

It is instructive to note what the epilogue is not. It does not provide historical information or predictions about the future. Rather, it goes back to the purpose of calling the Christians to remain faithful, underscoring our point that this is the central purpose of the book of Revelation.

At times we have portrayed the scenes as a sequence of movie images. Elsewhere, we have experienced them as a symphony, and at other times as a play on the stage. For the epilogue, the play is the appropriate image; Revelation means "to pull back the curtain." The play has ended, the curtain is closed, and Jesus comes on stage in front of the curtain for the epilogue. He speaks to those who have not yet responded to his call. He issues a tender invitation, later used for centuries as part of the Eucharist, "The Spirit and the Bride say, 'Come.' And let everyone who hears say, 'Come.' And let everyone who is thirsty come. Let everyone who wishes take the water of life as a gift." (22:17)

We have been privileged to look behind the curtain of time into the drama of eternity. We have seen a God of love who revealed himself in Jesus the Christ. We have seen how God has ruled throughout history, even when evil temporal rulers appear to be in control. We have noted the judgments that fall upon all who defy God. We have witnessed a final judgment that no person escapes. Portrayed for our inspiration and encouragement has been the glory of the New Jerusalem, the home of all as they have entered His kingdom. Now a longing invitation is extended: to him who is thirsty, come and drink freely of the water of life. The provision has been made. The invitation has been extended. Now all that remains is for us to respond.

Other members of heaven's cast come to stand by the side of Jesus in front of the curtain. There is a final word from the Lamb, "Surely I am coming soon." The saints and martyrs who stand with Christ answer, "Amen, come, Lord Jesus!"

And, finally, as we leave to go our way, there is the benediction. "The grace of the Lord Jesus be with all the saints. Amen." (22:21)

Questions for Discussion

1. What is your concept of heaven? How is it influenced by this vision at the end of Revelation?
2. Have you experienced church fellowship as "an outpost of heaven?"
3. The Judeo-Christian concept of history is linear; that is, there is a beginning and an ending. It begins as a garden and ends as another garden. Both Greek philosophy and eastern religions of Hinduism and Buddhism have viewed history as circular, a never ending cycle of beginnings and endings and new beginnings. Discuss these two views.
4. Can the specific images of life in heaven portrayed in Revelation be symbolic, pointing to a truth so deep it cannot be expressed in human terms—the ultimate and absolute reign of God?

AFTERWORD

Revelation as a Call to Sacred Activism

"... Humanity has come to the moment when it will have to choose between trying to play God, with the catastrophic results we see all around us, and trying to become what all the true mystical traditions know we can become—one with God through grace in life. This is a dangerous and yet wonderful and hopeful moment because if enough of us can choose the latter, the birth of a wholly new kind of human being, and so of a new world, is possible."

—Father Bede Griffiths[124]

---

124 A Roman Catholic mystic who lived in South India, quoted by Andrew Harvey in *The Hope: A Guide to Sacred Activism*, Hay House, 2009, p. 37.

The Church and the Emerging Vision of World Community

The turmoil at the core of our common life in America and elsewhere is a struggle to find a new meaning and a new approach to dealing with the many problems facing our world today. We are experiencing what is at heart a religious ferment in which a new world view is emerging from the womb of our collective unconscious. This is the big story of our day. It is the picture of our "spaceship earth" without borders, or Gaia, where all humanity and all living beings share a common destiny. This vision releases Christians from narrow perspectives and ethnocentric proclamations that claim God is on our side at the expense of others. The vision permits us to learn from all religious traditions while sharing our own "good news" of the gospel. This is the full-blown vision for the Church.

The fearful mass of people who do not understand the evolutionary tide that is pulling us toward our destiny in God's plan shrink back into isolationism. They espouse beliefs and values of a by-gone era, with a bizarre, sensationalized, literalist vision of end times that makes no sense in an age of science and global perspective.

The quest for our new foundation of understanding is emerging. Eighty percent of the people in our country believe in God. This is a big story. But how do we relate that belief to what is happening in the world around us? What does it mean to believe in God? For people of faith, our religion is the agency by which we make sense of what is happening in our world. Our challenge is to align our faith with a new vision of what God is doing in the world.

The Focus of the Church's Vision: Jesus

We go back, as always, to the man, Jesus of Nazareth. We look at his life and teaching, and we are convinced that he exemplified the best in humanity. We conclude that the best in humanity expresses the nature of God. So we believe that Jesus is like God. The tears of Jesus are the compassion of God. The anger of Jesus is the wrath of God, and the selfless sacrifice of Jesus' life reveals the deepest truth about the love of God. As Jesus was busy teaching, healing, proclaiming the coming of the kingdom of God on earth and declaring signs of the kingdom among the people, so our task is to look for and proclaim these signs in our day. We pray and work for the coming of God's kingdom on earth as it is in heaven. And we pray and work believing!

Jesus' life of love could not be destroyed by the forces of evil. The resurrection was a joyous witness to the eternal nature of humanity's relationship with God. The eternal God who is love lives forever and assures us that we live forever with Her/Him. But the vision taught by Jesus and the example of his life cannot be destroyed either. When he prayed, "Your kingdom come, Your will be done, on earth as it is in heaven," (Matthew 6:10) his was not an idle prayer. He prayed with passion, believing this kingdom could and should be realized on earth.

The focus of Jesus is to create transformed individuals who fully love God and fully love their neighbors. When Jesus was asked, "'Teacher, which commandment in the law is the greatest?' He said to him, 'You shall love the Lord your God with all your heart, and with all your soul, and with all your mind.' This is the greatest and first commandment. And a second is like it: 'You shall love your neighbor as yourself.' On these two commandments hang all the law and the prophets.'" (Matthew 22:36-40)

The practical effect of these laws fully at work in an individual or church group[125] is to ignite what Andrew Harvey calls "sacred activism."[126] This kind of

---

125 The Church of the Saviour in Washington D.C. (http://inwardoutward.org/the-church-of-the-saviour/) is structured on the insight that Christians are called to be on both a sacred "inward journey" and participate in a mission-based "outward journey" in order to love both God and neighbor in a meaningful way. Hence the requirement for membership that each person belong to a "mission group" with a commitment to inward spiritual practices and a specific project of serving others. I was privileged to be a member of this community for some ten years and experienced its power to transform individuals and to accomplish seemingly impossible tasks of service to the larger community and the world.

126 For a more detailed development of the concept of sacred activism, I recommend Andrew Harvey's book *The Hope: A Guide to Sacred Activism*, Hay House, 2009. Harvey considers sacred activism as the fusion of the mystic's love for God with the activist's love for justice. From my Christian perspective, this correlates with Jesus' two commandments that contain all the law and the prophets. Although we arrive at this concept from different places, Harvey's concept of sacred activism is highly compatible

activism is aligned with God's purpose for humanity as envisioned in Revelation, empowered by inner alignment with and participation in the larger cosmic community as described in Revelation. Oppressive personal, social, and economic orders are transformed and re-formed on the foundation of communion with God and love for others. This was the challenge in Revelation as Christians struggled within their own churches and faced the oppression and persecution of the Roman Empire. This is the challenge in our time as we build our communities of faith and confront the many seemingly insurmountable problems and perils of our world today.

Keys to the New Story

This vision of Revelation holds keys to the new story of the kingdom of God breaking into our world now, seeking birth in our midst. It is an old story, but new insight breaks forth from God's Word when humanity is faced with new challenges. What is the core of the vision? God rules. God's plan for the ages is taking shape. This is not a sectarian plan that includes only a small group of fundamentalists but excludes everyone else. It is a magnificent plan in which God wills to bring every nation and tribe and people together in a joyous community of humanity.

An ancient prophet held the vision, "The earth will be full of the knowledge of the Lord as the waters

---

with and enriching to my interpretation of the book of Revelation and its relevance to our calling as Christians today.

cover the sea." (Isaiah 11:9b) And Jesus himself said, "And I, when I am lifted up from the earth, will draw all people to myself." (John 12:32)

This is the real, literal world for which we hope and pray. We are called to live in the gap between what is and what ought to be—and then to spend our lives working to close that gap.

When we affirm that Christ puts all things under his feet, we believe he is stamping out small thinking, partisan advantage, self-centered power struggles, and the rich taking advantage of the poor. He is calling us to world community because he is the God of all humanity. By this call he is saying it is intolerable to have a world community with a small gold coast of very wealthy nations and a great world slum in the developing world alongside, with increasing spreads between the very wealthy and the poor.

When we look honestly at our world with discerning hearts of love we may be appropriately overwhelmed with anger. The trees in the Amazon jungle are being systematically cut to make room for plantation pastureland. At the same time we are told by atmospheric scientists that this large concentrated forest is essential to providing adequate atmosphere around planet earth. We see our atmosphere being polluted, so that our children will experience ever more extreme drought, flood, environmental degradation and rising ocean levels. This immeasurable harm could be mitigated even now—if we accepted the call to respect God's earth. Our food is being poisoned with chemical and biological agents, and our people are suffering and dying from cancer and a multitude of other health problems. The rich are getting obscenely rich and the poor are getting more desperate, while the middle class is shrinking.

Revelation shows in vivid imaginary the wrath of God. Seven bowls of God's wrath are poured out on a third of the earth as calls to repent. When humanity continues blindly along the path of destruction, God in His/Her wrathful mercy must destroy all of the structures of evil that harm so many people. Revelation gives us powerful imaginary depicting the Dragon, the Serpent, and Satan with his power to block necessary change—personified in our time as corporate-fed powers that maintain and expand the embedded unjust social and economic structures, designed to benefit the wealthy and powerful, regardless of harm to those not in power.

So, a vital step in the transformation of the earth into the kingdom of God is to allow ourselves to become angry. God's saints need a white hot anger—the kind that takes a whip and drives moneychangers out of the temple. It is not enough to say prayers and prepare for heaven. We must do more. We must confront the "principalities and powers" entrenched in our social and economic system.

Those who become committed activists for the kingdom of justice and peace and love are God's agents for a literal redemption of the world. These are the servants of God who live with unspeakable joy, heavenly joy, as their labor is supported by the saints of heaven and the angels—all the heavenly hosts—who long more than anything else to see a saved and redeemed earth.

We are well aware that "the sisterhood and brotherhood of humanity" does not come easily and may never come completely. Always we must be alert to shadow forces at work within each of us, in our social order, and yes, in the Church. The struggle goes on, but the vision of a world in which we learn to live together in peace with justice, inspired by those who are committed to Christ and his kingdom, is more vivid and closer to realization now than ever, even as deep shadows fall over our world.

We affirm that the God of the universe we worship is the same God who is worshipped by Jews, Muslims, Hindus, Buddhists, and other religious people. As a Christian, I affirm my devotion to Jesus Christ. But I also acknowledge that God is at work among all of us in the common family of humanity.

It is as if God is saying, "It was my intention from the beginning of time that humans should live together with respect, honor, and fairness. Since I love all people unconditionally, it is my purpose for the ages that all people should care for each other. Now, at this time in history, the world is suffering under innumerable problems brought about by human ignorance, selfishness, and greed. Human spiritual and moral development has not kept pace with technological development. Finally, my patience is running out. Either humanity must learn to live together as I intended from the beginning, or they will destroy themselves with the instruments of technology that I have placed in their hands. I have given warning signs. People are aware of the holes in the atmosphere caused by ozone depletion. They have experienced partial judgments. They know that nuclear weapons have already wrought havoc, with massive death and suffering passed to future generations through genetic damage. Nuclear weapons and nuclear energy accidents can create a dark winter in which the sun is blotted out for decades and life on earth is destroyed. The people understand that they can fish the oceans until they are depleted, because it has happened with some species. They can pollute the air until it cannot be breathed. I have given my people knowledge of good and evil."

God has provided a community of concerned and committed people—the Church—for the struggle. The churches provide fellowships of caring where we can grow in our inner lives of prayer and relationship with God, grow in faith, hope, and love—and undertake more effective works for confronting the principalities and powers and for building God's kingdom on earth.

This is our community—the one Jesus called together as the place for us to undertake and support each other in this sacred activism. Christ still stands among the churches, lighting the candles of hope and assuring humanity of victory when his followers act with devotion, faith, and passion.

We, as Christians, along with serious seekers in all religions, are invited to participate in the main events of history. Indeed, we are called to make history, to reveal the love offered by Jesus, and to proclaim the vision of God's rule over the world. This is the message of Revelation. It speaks personally and powerfully to each of us, as we rejoice with him who rides the white horse to victory!

This I believe.

APPENDIX 1

A BRIEF HISTORY OF APOCALYPTIC LITERATURE

Revelation is written in the style of apocalyptic literature. This style of writing, with its vivid imagery, was familiar to the Christians of Asia Minor (for whom it was originally written), but it is foreign to most of us. I write this appendix, not to be exhaustive, but to provide some background and context so that we can better understand Revelation. This is an "extra" for those who want to take the study an added step.

Helpful Definitions

The word "providence" means to set within the plan of God. The Latin "pro" means "before" and "video" is "to see." Providence is God planning and knowing what will happen prior to the actual events. It is God planning ahead. Revelation depicts history as under the sovereignty of God. Someone is in the driver's seat of history. We are ruled by the providence of God.

The Greek word "eschaton" is used by theologians to describe end things. In a narrative story it is the conclusion or ending. Eschatology, then, is God guiding history to its final end. Eschatology is the counterpart to creation. God created the world and human beings by willful acts. God is not only the Alpha, but also the Omega. The doctrine of the end of the world within Christianity should not be perceived as gloomy or pessimistic, but rather as a joyous hope to be celebrated.

Biblical writers believed implicitly that God has a plan for the world. He is directing history, while still providing for human freedom and thus human involvement in that plan. The prophets of the Old Testament portrayed the coming of a Messiah who would judge sinfulness and save the faithful. Some of these prophets saw this happening within history. Others held an apocalyptic view. They believed that God would intervene from outside of history to overturn evil rulers and end history in a cataclysm.

Apocalypse is, then, a certain way of thinking about eschatology. Apocalyptic writings portray a sudden and cataclysmic end of history. The ultimate power of evil is pitted against God. This way of thinking gained credence in eras when common people felt helpless against powerful rulers. Generally, apocalyptic thinking was an expression of faith by people who were politically powerless and oppressed. When they evaluated the social order they could not discern the goodness of God being expressed toward them, and yet they were God's people who affirmed that goodness. They asked, "What power do we have to keep Caesar from working his will?" or the counter question, "Is God faithful?" At that point they turned to apocalyptic explanations to testify that, while the world situation seemed hopeless, there was a mighty "nevertheless...."

Hebrew History of Apocalyptic Literature

As this literature developed it drew heavily on ancient myths from Babylon and Canaan in which powerful demons opposed God. In time, the stories evolved into God and the angels on one side and Satan and his demons on the other. The belief emerged in eschatological thinking that evil was so bad that no mere human was capable of causing it.

To more fully understand Revelation as an apocalyptic book it is necessary for us to go back at least 300 years before the birth of Jesus and see how the concept of Antichrist developed from Anti-Messiah. People earnestly hoped for the Messiah and predicted he would rescue Israel from the forces of evil. At the same time they grew increasingly afraid of powerful enemies who threatened their destruction.

There are 15 surviving books of Jewish apocalypse, all written between 250 B.C. and 150 A.D. All of them follow a similar literary form. Each is a divine oracle communicated to a human prophet, usually by way of an angel. The author is often anonymous, but takes the name of a well-known leader of the past. The books Enoch, Ezra, and Daniel are primary examples.

Scholars refer to the era in which these books were written as "the second temple era," the period between the return of Israel from the Babylonian captivity, when the temple was rebuilt, and 70 A.D., when the temple was again destroyed. The Qumran scrolls, discovered in the 1940s, also date from this era. They were written by scholars in an ascetic community that lived in the wilderness near Jericho in the days of Jesus. Their scrolls were wrapped and placed in clay jars and then hidden in caves just before the community was destroyed. These scrolls, in the tradition of apocalyptic thinking, indicate a strong belief in an Anti-Messiah, but they did not include a complete book of apocalypse like the book of Revelation.

The book from this period that made its way into the Old Testament canon was Daniel, written between 167 and 164 B.C. Much of the book of Revelation is based on both the ideas and the language of Daniel. As in the other books of this type, there is a crisis, a final judgment, and a reward for one's deeds, either good or bad. God's enemy is routed and there is final vindication for those who suffer persecution. A Savior rises up at the end, and there is the hope that the faithful will not see death, but will be translated into heavenly beings.

The four beasts of Daniel were Babylon, the Medes, the Persians and the Greeks (Hellenists). These powerful kingdoms had overrun and conquered Israel over a period of some two hundred years. At the time Daniel was written, there was a crisis in the life of Israel. Antiochus IV in 169 B.C. captured Jerusalem and plundered the city. In 167 B.C. he banned Jewish religious practice. This edict led to the outbreak of a war known as the "Maccabean revolt." In December of

164 B.C., Judas Maccabee took back the city of Jerusalem and purified the temple, which had been desecrated.

In Daniel, Chapters 7-12, Antiochus IV is portrayed as "little horn" who remains an evil human king. His efforts to Hellenize the city are described in 1 Maccabees 1:11-16 and in 2 Maccabees 4:7-17. The author of Daniel drew on ancient myths and vivid imagery from the lore of Babylon and Canaan. Much of this imagery then, in turn, made its way into Revelation to describe yet another evil ruler.

The Daniel story was built on ancient myths handed down and refined across centuries of telling. They are both primordial and archetypical. One is the ancient combat myth. This story relates the struggle between a god and a monster of chaos at the time of creation. But in Revelation the myth is not retold simply to add color or repeat an ancient story. John adapts the story, expands it and transforms it into a vehicle for his message.

Some of us become uncomfortable with the word "myth" in the context of sacred scripture. A myth is a story intended to explain a sacred meaning or truth. The story is not historical, but it does point to a basic reality. Thus, the story of Adam and Eve is a myth, a story that reveals the truth of God as the Creator. It reveals how God intended good for humanity, but we chose and still choose to do evil. The story reveals the truth that we are made in the image of God. We are in historical and scientific trouble when we take a myth literally. If we accept it as a vehicle for understanding truth, it illuminates the dark horizon like the rising of the morning sun. When the human mind grapples with the mystery of beginnings and endings, myth becomes the best vehicle for conveying truth.

Intertwined with myth is legend. Legend claims to have happened in history. Legend is partly factual but the cloth of fact has been embroidered into a more powerful story, using imagination to teach a lesson or to instill pride or patriotism. Usually in legend there is an intermingling of history and myth.

In summary, the apocalypse of Revelation is a combination of myth and legend from Hebrew history. The origin lies in historical memory. The Christian prophet, John, sought to explain current events and project a future outcome. In Daniel we saw how a harsh foreign sovereign subjugated the Jewish religion and desecrated the temple. We saw a leader of Israel rise up, lead a rebellion, and win back the land and the right to practice their religion. To explain the meaning, the writer drew on ancient mythology and 400 years of Jewish history. This history, with its profound insight conveyed through myth and legend, is incorporated into Revelation but in such a way that new truth is revealed about God and His Christ.

In Revelation the imagery is used to create a futurist legend. The opposition of Rome becomes part of a primordial struggle between good and evil. This struggle for survival of the churches is presented as a contrast between "this evil age" and "the age to come." Once more earth is set against heaven. Christ rides against the powerful beast in the form of Caesar Domitian, and in the end the forces of God prevail.

New Testament Apocalypse

The concept of the Christ's return is present in other parts of the New Testament. The earliest book was probably 1 Thessalonians, written by Paul around 50 A.D., before the gospel writings were assembled. Paul seeks to answer the questions of when Christ will return and what happens to Christians who die before his return. We are warned not to set a date for his return; Christ will come unexpectedly, "like a thief in the night." The emphasis is on watchfulness. There is no mention of an "Antichrist."

In 2 Thessalonians, written years later, there is an account of "the final enemy," but again the term "Antichrist" is not used. Those who describe an Antichrist use 2 Thessalonians 2:1-12 as the basis for their post-Biblical concept of the Antichrist as a political figure, with the motifs of rebellion, blasphemy and deception. They claim that there is to be a leader in the last days who acts with energy and the power of Satan. This human opponent grapples with and is defeated by the risen Lord.

This post-Biblical speculation falsely interprets Paul's message to the church. Paul refers to earlier advice he gave the church when he was visiting in person, regarding a false teacher with great power who corrupts the church and hurts the larger society. Those who spin the theory that an "Antichrist" being described here do so in the pattern of Old Testament apocalyptic writing, not New Testament canonical scripture.

In 1 John and 2 John, the only New Testament books where the term "antichrist" is used,[127] the term describes a false teacher within the Church, not a political figure. Internal problems increased in the churches as time went by and Christ had not returned. The deceivers and false prophets were considered "antichrist."

Nero and Domitian as Antichrist

This chapter has presented a brief background for apocalyptic thinking and for the second coming of Christ. These ancient references and New Testament writings form the basis for the next 2,000 years of predicting the second coming of Christ and of identifying the "Antichrist" either as an evil political leader or a heretical teacher within the church.

One would think that Vespasian, who ruled when Jerusalem was destroyed, would be part of the Antichrist legend. Rather, it was Nero who was first perceived as the Antichrist, probably because he was first to claim divine status. Nero was an evil and cruel megalomaniac. Because he claimed divinity, Nero tried to justify his right to rule with an iron fist. When poor planning and bad judgment led to chaos, he blamed it all on the Christians. Finally, at the bitter end, the Roman public realized that Nero was making excuses and "scapegoating" the Christians for his own failures. Nero then fell on his own sword and killed himself.

---

127 1 John 2:18; 1 John 2:22; 1 John 4:3; 2 John 1:7

Soon after his demise rumors spread that Nero was still alive. Some said he had fled to the province of Pathia where he was gathering an army. People believed he planned to return, destroy his opponents and continue his persecution of Christians.

In Revelation Domitian is the Beast, later called the Antichrist, but he is portrayed as having within him the spirit of Nero. In Revelation the figure of Nero is the Beast from the abyss. Also, one of the seven heads of the Beast from the Sea is depicted as Nero. The head that received a fatal wound was restored to life.

Christ and Antichrist in Church History

There was intermittent persecution of Christians through the second century. For such an age the book of Revelation had its greatest meaning. While scholars questioned and evaluated the book, common people lived into its message of faithfulness and hope. This century became an age of spectacular success for the Church as it spread across the empire. Imperceptibly, by day and by night, the gospel of Christ penetrated the pagan society at all levels until in 325 A.D. Constantine, through the prayers of his Christian mother, became a Christian. The Emperor then led the Church toward becoming the official religion of the empire.

Self-styled prophets have predicted the end of the world at every major historical date since New Testament times. Hippolyton, a disciple of Irenaeus in the second century, drew up a time table and predicted the end of the world in 500 A.D. The majority of Christians in the second century rejected this scenario, believing the end would come much sooner. However, during the fourth and fifth centuries his writings convinced many within the Church.

Augustine (354-430) tried to diffuse expectations of an imminent arrival of the end of the world. In the era in which he lived many persons were perceived as "Antichrist," especially leaders of the Germanic barbarians who conquered Rome. The great theologian offered an anti-millennial interpretation of Revelation and understood Christ versus Antichrist as the struggle between good and evil that goes on in the life of every Christian. In his classic book, *The City of God*, Augustine wrote of multiple Antichrists. All evildoers, slave dealers, cheaters and drunkards are Antichrist.

Augustine's interpretation of Revelation became the orthodox position of the Roman Catholic Church and continues until now to be one of the primary positions of both Catholicism and mainstream Protestantism. Rather than projecting all evil situations onto a cosmic evil person, Augustine taught us to see this very real tendency to sin as a constant battle within each of us.

Premillennialism, with its scenario of a last great battle between God and Satan at Armageddon, declined during the fourth century. When the empire became officially Christian, Rome, the Woman in Scarlet, no longer appeared as a threat to the churches. When Christ did not return after three hundred years, people sought a more symbolic view and focused more on making the world into a Christian kingdom of God.

In the period between 500 and 1000 A.D., the Antichrist was most often identified with the rise of Islamic power, the invasion of Spain and the capture of Jerusalem. Islamic conquerors made the holy temple into a Muslim mosque. The Moorish invasion of Spain came in the early ninth century. At first the hordes who poured in were perceived primarily as political and military enemies. But as they became better known, the religious message of Islam was studied seriously, and Islam was understood more as a Christian heresy than as a separate religion. Yet the rise of Islam became for many the sign that Christ would come soon to defeat this Antichrist. Mohammed, the false prophet, was the final enemy.

The crusades were launched, in part, to rescue the Holy City, Jerusalem, from the wicked Muslims. The first crusade set out in 1095 under Gregory VII. It was billed as a rescue mission. In fact, it was part of a papal foreign policy based on the hope that a common enemy would unify the Christian world under the pope. The crusades really got under way under Pope Urban II. His speech launching the second crusade is instructive. He called on his warriors to retake Jerusalem so that the Antichrist could then attack them. The pope explained that the end of the world would not come until the Jews returned to their homeland and Christians had routed the Muslims. He proclaimed, "The end of the world is near, even if the pagans are no longer being converted to God.... According to the prophets, before the coming of Antichrist, it is first necessary that the Christian Empire be renewed in these parts, either through you, or through those whom God pleases, so that the head of all evil who will have his imperial throne there may find some nourishment of faith against which he might fight."

Through the centuries between 1000 and 1500, many writers made predictions about the end of the world in their times. The debates and controversies were alive and well. Two examples from this era illustrate the intense interest in Revelation. The first is an early saint, Bernard of Clairvaux (1090-1153). Bernard was a devout man with a magnetic personality. He had a deep inner life of prayer; he was concerned with church reform and renewal. We know about him because he was also a gifted writer and helped form a new religious order called the Cistercians.

Bernard divided the history of the Church into four eras. There was the Apostolic Age, followed by the Age of the Rise and Formation of the Roman Catholic Church. The era in which he lived was the third age, a time of internal hypocrisy. The fourth and final era was at hand. Antichrist would rise and Christ would come again.

My second example is none other than Christopher Columbus. The explorer was on a religious mission centered in his understanding of the book of Revelation. He wrote *The Book of Prophesy,* a compilation of apocalyptic revelations based on his belief that the end of the world was near. But before Christ could come again certain events must transpire. First, the gospel must be preached throughout the world. Second, a World Emperor must be chosen. In his mind, the Catholic monarchs, Ferdinand and Isabella, were these chosen ones. Third, these monarchs would lead the crusade to free the Holy Land from Muslim rule. Columbus saw his role as that of opening the door to all the lands of the world. He had a mystical, religion-driven mission of exploration as God's agent so that Christ might come again.

In summary, the concept of the "second coming of Christ" in the clouds, followed by a final great battle against the perceived most evil ruler of the era, has been present throughout Christian history, though its Biblical validity is questionable. Details about the identity of the "Antichrist" changed with almost every generation. A large segment of the Christian community has always found it more appealing to have Christ step in to end history than to work unceasingly themselves for the coming of God's kingdom on earth as it is in heaven.

APPENDIX 2

END TIMES IN THE CONTEMPORARY CHURCH

There is a deafening silence about the end of time in contemporary Catholicism and among most mainline Protestants. To be sure, there are scholarly books being published on Revelation, but little if any of this scholarship filters down to ordinary, thoughtful lay people. However, many fundamentalist Christians make the rise of a final Antichrist and the Second Coming of Christ the focus of their faith, with constant writing and preaching on the subject.

Because of the relative silence on one side and the steady barrage of books and preaching and media attention on the other, millions of people are drawn into a belief system that deeper understanding would not support. This book is presented as one attempt to speak to, and perhaps for, many mainline Christians. A Pew Research Center survey taken April of 2010 found that roughly half of Christians in the United States believe that Christ will literally return to earth in the next 40 years. (Twenty-seven percent believe that this is definite and 20% believe that it is probable.)

The Fundamentalist Perspective

I now turn to the teachings of the fundamentalists, beginning with a brief history.

John Nelson Darby, an English preacher, pioneered modern fundamentalism. He came to the United States in the 1840s and spent the rest of his life here preaching a new theology based on Revelation. His movement grew after the Civil War, when there was widespread poverty and pessimism. His teachings got a big boost in 1909 with the publication of the Scofield Reference Bible and with the development of many Bible institutes that prepared men for ministry based on a narrowly focused Bible training.

Darby called himself a "Dispensationalist." The term refers to the theory that God has dispensed the divine plan for history in seven distinct and successive stages called "dispensations." He taught that the end of history was at hand, and the seventh and last dispensation was the return of Christ, followed by his thousand-year reign, the millennium.

While there were many subplots and variations on the main thesis, generally these believers were "premillennialists" who taught there will be three distinct eras related to end times: the rapture, the tribulation, and the millennium.

The rapture is the physical coming of Christ in the sky. This doctrine is based on a literal reading of 1 Thessalonians 4:16-17, in which Paul wrote that the faithful who are still alive will be caught up with the dead saints, who will break forth from their tombs, to meet Christ in the air. Again, Paul sought to assure the Christians that those of their numbers who had died would not be penalized when Christ returned.

The tribulation is a seven year period following the rapture, during which time Antichrist will rule the earth. First, Israel and then the whole world will be subject to persecution. The Antichrist will be a human dictator in the mold of a Hitler who will rule the world through a renewed Roman Empire. This is based on a reading of Daniel, Ezekiel and Revelation. (Revelation 19:19-20) However, Darby taught that the Christians who are alive will be translated and carried to heaven, thus avoiding the horrors of the tribulation.

At the end of the seven years of terror, Christ will again return to the earth and fight in a final great battle at Armageddon. He will defeat Antichrist and all of his hosts, casting him and his cohorts into the everlasting lake of fire.

When that event is completed, Christ will begin the reign of a thousand years on earth. Presumably, the saints will have waited in an intermediate location and will return to earth with Christ for this millennial reign. When the thousand years is completed, earth's history will end with the final judgment, followed by God's reign forever in heaven with Christ and all the redeemed.

To many thoughtful Christians there are serious problems with this projection of end things. First, we are reminded that this uses of the term and even the concept of Antichrist is entirely non-Biblical. The few times it was used in the New Testament, It referred to false teachers within the church. Second, it is based on a patchwork of scripture passages pieced together to form a pattern that could just as well be reconfigured in a different way. Indeed, if one takes Revelation, Chapters 19 and 20 literally and in the order in which they are presented, a very different saga unfolds.

Third, the scenario defies reason and leaves logistical questions unanswered. For example, what happens to the "saved" on earth and the dead who have been raised during the seven years of rapture? What happens to the seven billion (or more) people on earth who are not Christians during the thousand years of Christ's reign on earth? Will they all be converted? Or will they be killed and sent to hell?

Fourth, there are additional theological problems. Would the loving, saving Christ leave the world to be dominated by Satan for seven years without a smidgen of godliness on the earth during that time? Would Jesus, who refused to take the sword during his earthly life, become a general leading a conquering army against the rest of the world during a literal battle of Armageddon?

Finally, it should be noted that historically Christians have believed they are not given special consideration for avoiding unpleasantness but may be called upon to endure, as did the Christians in the first century. However, the latter day dispensationalists have created the powerful hope among their followers that they will not have to face death, nor be subject to the persecution of the Antichrist. Rather, they will wait things out in heaven while the remainder of humanity is tormented and destroyed. This optimistic innovation of having the Christians avoid suffering is seen by some as a desire for cheap grace, quite the opposite of the message of Revelation.

After trying to work within established denominations, the fundamentalists, strengthened by Bible colleges and institutes, took a more independent course in the twentieth century. Many local congregations pulled away from their parent denominations to form new fundamentalist counterpoint Baptist or Presbyterian churches, or new denominations.

The early movement lacked a realistic way to connect current political conditions to their Biblical prophecy. A decisive event occurred for them with the emergence of the state of Israel. The first signpost was seen at the end of World War I. To these fundamentalist Christians the most significant aspect of World War I was not the epic struggle to defeat Germany that cost millions of lives on both sides, but rather it was the so-called Balfour Declaration of 1917. Lord Balfour, the British Foreign Secretary, wrote, "His Majesty's government views with favor the establishment in Palestine of a national home for the Jewish people." For the premillennialists, this was the beginning of a clear case of biblical prophecy being fulfilled.

Leading exponents of Dispensationalism today believe there was a lapse in the fulfillment of Biblical prophecy between the writing of Revelation and 1948, the year the state of Israel was established. All prophesies left unfulfilled had to wait for completion until the return of the Jews to Palestine. Only then could the apocalyptic clock begin to tick again, leading to the end of time.

Hal Lindsay is a prototype of contemporary premillennialism. He serves as a good example because his books have sold most widely. Lindsay was educated at the Dallas Theological Seminary, often called "the Vatican of Premillennialism." Lindsay served as a campus minister at UCLA in the 1960s and then returned to the Dallas faculty. In 1970 he published an apocalyptic book with the title *The Last Great Planet Earth.* It was the best seller of all books published in the 1970s and is still in print, having reached total sales of more than 25,000,000 copies.

Lindsay's book contains little that is new; it is the standard premillennial scenario. The beginning of the Jewish state of Israel is said to be the sign that we are living in the last generation. The European Economic Community is equated with Rome in the book of Revelation. Lindsay sees a ten nation United States of Europe (the beast with ten heads) that will become the power base for the Antichrist, "the Future Fuhrer." This leader will sign a peace treaty with Israel that will lead to the rebuilding of the temple. He will be revealed as Antichrist when he is seriously wounded in the head and miraculously recovers. Associated with him will be a Jewish false prophet who will compel everyone to worship the dictator. Those who refuse, especially 144,000 newly converted Jews, will suffer persecution.

Another writer with a slightly different interpretation is a mentor, friend and colleague of Lindsay, John F. Walvoord. Dr. Walvoord served as President of Dallas Theological Seminary from 1952 to 1986. He has written many books on Biblical prophecy but is best known for *Armageddon, Oil, and the Middle East Crisis: What the Bible Says about the Future of the Middle East and End of Western Civilization,* written in 1974 and revised in 1990 in light of new historical developments in the Middle East. The publisher claims to have sold a million copies in two months during the Gulf War.

Walvoord's book is centered more on a Mediterranean confederacy that becomes the new Roman Empire. In his analysis, the leader of this emerging political power will force Israel to make peace with the Arabs. This will end regular time and begin the tribulation, the final seven years of history. Walvoord believes there will be an apostate super-church formed in the last days – a Council of Churches consisting of the Roman Catholic Church, the World Council of Churches, and the Greek Orthodox Church. This Council composed of "apostate pretenders" is understood to be the Harlot riding on the Beast in Revelation.

During the first three-and-a-half-year reign, a divine intervention will destroy a Russian invasion of Israel (Ezekiel 38-39). This invasion will be conducted by cavalry, as stated in Ezekiel, because of a shortage of oil in the Middle East that will prohibit the use of motor vehicles. Christ will descend on the Mount of Olives. Then Antichrist will be cast into hell. Both Jews and Gentiles will be judged and then the millennium will begin.

These literalist Bible school prophets form their views of end times using contemporary events and fitting them into select Bible passages, then claiming they are revealed truth based on inerrancy of scripture.

Prominent fundamentalist preachers, including Pat Robertson and the late Jerry Falwell, pledged their support for the state of Israel. They offered as Biblical grounds for this support the belief that Jews must return to Israel and then be converted to Christ before the final events of history can transpire.

The state of Israel welcomed this support because it provided political cover for Israel in the Congress of the United States. Israel received the televangelists with great fanfare, but the Israeli leaders have no intention of converting to Christianity.

This I Believe

If you have read this book and followed the commentary you are well aware that my own view is at wide variance with all of the premillennial thinking so popular today. My sad conclusion is that their interpretations are not Biblical. They may be promulgated by persons who sincerely believe them, although some sensationalist preachers perhaps fudge their own commitment to truth, knowing the power of frightening predictions to generate followings.

The dilemma faced by those of us in mainline churches includes our distaste for polemic with opponents. And yet the book of Revelation points to the constant need to isolate heretical teachings from the Body of Christ. It is an unpleasant dilemma we need to face for the sake of the millions of unsuspecting Christians who look up to these latter-day preachers and self-proclaimed prophets. There is "a more excellent way" – the path of personal commitment, joyous service, and deeper interpretation of scripture.

ACKNOWLEDGEMENTS

I acknowledge the great company of scholars, both living and dead, who have done research, study and writing to help the living interpret the book of Revelation. Equally important are the mystics and saints who have lived into union with God and love for humanity, so they could verify the reality of Revelation and inspire us to claim for ourselves the joys that are found on its pages.

Most important for this enterprise is Susanna McCan, my daughter, who contributed her own deep insight into Revelation, based on her long term meditation practice and in-depth study of the world religions with their common archetypes. Susanna managed the entire process of preparing the book for publication through her company, Flying Swan Publications. She served as my primary editor, worked with me on the interior design of the book, and handled all the formatting and other technical aspects of the publishing process. She also envisioned with me the concept for the cover art and helped me select the images. Jason Fleming, my stepson, a professional artist and graphic designer, then brought the vision for the cover to life.

To both of them, thank you.

ABOUT THE AUTHOR

Dr. McCan graduated from Yale University Divinity School and earned his Ph.D. from the University of Edinburg. He continued his formal education as a Visiting Scholar with faulty status at Harvard University.

Dr. McCan is an ordained Southern Baptist minister who has held pastorates in three churches. He founded and served as President of Dag Hammarskjold College, where the students, faculty and Board members from diverse cultures formed a miniature world community.

His career in government included executive positions in the Office of Economic Opportunity, the U.S. Office of Education, the Woodrow Wilson International Center for Scholars, and the U.S. Agency for International Development.

Dr. McCan also served as Assistant Professor of Political Ethics at Wesley Theological Seminary and as an Associate at the Churches Center for Theology and Public Policy, a Washington, D.C. think tank sponsored by mainline Protestant churches and the Roman Catholic Church to develop public policy positions.

Previous books by Dr. McCan include *A Vision of Victory*, 1959; *World Economy and World Hunger*, 1982; *Justice for Gays and Lesbians: Crisis and Challenge in the Episcopal Church*, 2006; *Citizen's Guide to Health Care Reform: Understanding the Affordable Care Act*, 2012.

Made in the USA
Charleston, SC
17 November 2013